Glasgow Buses

by
Stuart Little M.C.I.T.

Transport Publishing Co Ltd : Glossop : Derbyshire : England

Glasgow's New City Road in 1930. In this view, the hitherto indomitable position of the tramcar is being challenged as a two-year-old open staircase Leyland Titan pursues a new Cowieson-bodied AEC Regent, No. 254, working on GCT service 8 from Ruchill to Merrylee Road. Another Titan is visible in front of the Standard tram, typical of the fleet at that date. The Austin Twenty in the foreground had much the same air of sturdy reliability, as the two buses behind it, but was if anything, more staid.

© TPC/STTS

March 1990

ISBN 086317 145 1

Typeset and produced for the Publishers by Mopok Graphics, 128 Pikes Lane, Glossop Printed in England

Contents

Introduction

The City of Glasgow had locally-controlled public transport of one form or another from 1894. Over 90 years later, local authority control was released to 'private' companies when the Transport Act 1985 was enacted in October 1986. It seems an appropriate time, therefore, to set on record the bus fleet used by Glasgow Corporation Transport and its subsequent authorities which provided the city's population with a motorbus service from 1924.

In trying to capture the story of the tramcars' rubber-tyred companion I am mindful that the bus has never been seen with affection, since in many eyes it was the tram's predator! Energetic managers like Messrs Dalrymple and Fitzpayne proved that the tram and bus could operate and complement each other. The sheer volume of buses purchased, the variety of the designs, experimental ideas and characteristic operating conditions in this part of the United Kingdom have, however, left their mark: from the solid-tyred Commers of 1924 through to the largest fleet of Leyland Atlanteans in the world.

Glasgow Corporation Transport was taken over by the Greater Glasgow Passenger Transport Executive in 1973, and, following local government reform in Scotland, by Strathclyde Regional Council in 1975. The Transport Act 1985 has made necessary the formation of a wholly-owned subsidiary 'Strathclyde Buses Ltd' and the PTE relinquished direct bus operation in October 1986. Transport Acts, buses, colour schemes and passengers may wax and wane, but no matter. In this city, the principal carrier of its citizens will, I have no doubt, always be referred to as 'The Corporation Bus'.

Stuart Little, M.C.I.T.
January 1988

With the Royal Infirmary in the background, Daimler D5 travels towards Glasgow Cross. The city's mediaeval beginnings lie here in Castle Street at Cathedral Square. While the remains of the Bishop's Palace are still some years away from excavation and display, more recent evidence of the former High Street tram route and newly erected trolleybus overhead dates this scene to around 1951.

Acknowledgements

The author expresses his sincere thanks to the following individuals who, unstintingly, provided valuable help and encouragement in the compilation and production of this book:-

J. Clayson, J. Coats, B. Deans, A. Douglas, C. Dunbar, G. Ewing, J. Fender, I. Fraser, R. Grieves, G. Heaney, I. MacGregor, A. MacDonald, K. MacKay, R. F. Mack, R. Marshall, A. Millar, W. O'Neill, M. Roulston, I. Stewart, D. Thomson, J. Thompson, A. Townsin, W. Tuckwell, and D. Wilson. The assistance of the staff of the former Strathclyde PTE (Engineering and Press and Media Departments); The Mitchell Library, Glasgow; W. Alexander and Sons (Coachbuilders) Ltd; and the Glasgow Museum of Transport is also acknowledged.

Information is believed correct to October 1986. Any queries regarding information published should be addressed to the Scottish Tramway and Transport Society, PO Box 78, Glasgow, G3 6ER, and *not* to any individual person or company.

Bibliography

Commercial Motor; Motor Transport; Buses (formerly Buses Illustrated); A Handbook of GCT Motorbuses (STMS, 1970); Almost 50 But Not Quite (STMS, 1974); The PSV Circle: Motorbuses and Trolleybuses of the Scottish Municipalities (1962); Strathclyde PTE (PSV/Omnibus Society, 1985); British Double Deckers since 1942 — A. A. Townsin (I. Allan, 1965); The Best of British Buses Nos. 7 and 8 — A. A. Townsin (TPC, 1982); British Bus Fleets No. 20 — I. Maclean (I, Allan, 1963); Buses and Trolleybuses 1919-45 — D. Kaye (Blandford Press, 1970); Annual Reports of Glasgow Corporation Tramways/Transport (GCT), Greater Glasgow PTE and Strathclyde PTE.

Photo credits

Acknowledgement is made to the following sources and individuals for the use of photographic illustrations in this book:-

W. Alexander & Co (Coachbuilders) Ltd	29, 71 (lower right)
T. & R. Annan & Sons Ltd	7 (lower), 10
Author	Colour plates XI, XII, 54(centre left, lower), 59, 60, 62 (centre, lower right), 63(both), 69(lower), 76(upper, centre upper, lower), 78
Author's collection	7 (upper), 12(lower), 17(lower right), 20(upper), 22, 25(centre upper), 40(lower), 53(upper), 68
Commercial Motor	17(upper)
B. T. Deans	Colour plates III, X, 50 (lower left), 62(lower left)
A. J. Douglas	32(upper right), 69(centre right), 71(centre), 73 (both)
J. G. Fender	75(lower)
Glasgow Corporation Transport	6, 11(upper right), 15(lower), 16(centre), 23(upper left, lower), 28, 53(centre), 66(upper), 71(upper)
Glasgow Museum of Transport	51
Glasgow Museum of Transport collection	8(upper), 18, 46(lower), 70(upper), 79
R. L. Grieves	50(centre), 80
R. L. Grieves collection	9, 11(upper left), 15 (upper), 21(upper left), 32(upper left), 64(lower)
Greater Glasgow PTE/ Strathclyde PTE	54(upper, centre right), 56, 57, 58, 61, 75(upper, centre), 76(centre lower), 77
Hurst, Nelson Collection, courtesy J. H. Price	70(lower)

Leyland Motors	49(upper)
London Transport collection	26
I. MacGregor	Colour plate II
K. K. MacKay	17(centre right), 21(upper right, lower), 25(upper), 27(centre), 33(upper), 43, 45(upper)
R. F. Mack	30(upper, centre), 33(centre, lower), 34, 36(upper right), 37 (all), 39, 45(lower), 50(lower right)
R. Marshall	24, 25(centre lower, lower)
R. Marshall collection	16(lower), 20(centre left), 27(upper left), 64(upper)
A. Millar	49(lower)
Geo. Outram & Co Ltd	14, 66(lower)
R. B. Parr/STTS collection	50(upper)
W. A. C. Smith	46(upper right)
I. G. McM. Stewart	Cover drawing, 27(upper right), 42, 46(upper left)
I. G. McM. Stewart collection	69(centre left)
J. Thomson	Covers, Colour plates I, IV-IX, 17(lower left), 20(centre right), 21(centre), 30(lower), 32(upper centre), 35, 36(upper left), 40(centre), 44(all), 45(centre), 46(centre), 47, 65(both), 71(lower left)
Transport Publishing Company Ltd	2, 4, 8(lower), 12(upper), 13, 23(upper right)
D. G. Wilson	62(upper)
D. G. Wilson collection	31, 38, 40(upper), 41, 67, 69(upper)

Chapter one: The first ten years

On 19th August 1922, the Golden Jubilee of Glasgow's tramway system was celebrated. The Tramways Department was justifiably proud of the network which was the envy of many local authorities and within three years would serve a population approaching 1,300,000 in an area stretching from Airdrie in the east to Kilbarchan in the west. The electric tramcar fleet had grown from 21 single-deck 'Room and Kitchen' cars in 1898 to 1004 'Standard' trams by 1924, supplemented by 72 ex-Paisley District Tramways cars and fifteen from the Airdrie and Coatbridge company, both of whom had been taken over by Glasgow Corporation Tramways (GCT) in 1923, giving a total of over 270 street miles of tramway in the Greater Glasgow area and providing a service second to none. Integrated transport Clyde-wide is not new!

It was this very success which delayed any notion of running motorbuses long after their mechanical reliability had been proved by other operators. On paper, at least, the Corporation had powers granted to use motorbuses on extensions to existing tram routes (in 1905 and 1913) and did actually have a demonstration using a Tilling-Stevens vehicle in 1921. A Provisional Order in 1922 renewed these powers and widened the scope for future operations — also giving the Corporation powers to manufacture bus

chassis which were to remain unused.

After the Airdrie and Coatbridge system was acquired by the Tramways Department, it was decided to renew and double the existing track between the two Burghs. A replacement service of motorbuses would provide an ideal opportunity for a small-scale trial using such vehicles. By 1924, the task had begun to select the necessary fourteen buses and before long it was reported that the job was proving to be far from easy. At the time there was a bewildering range of both chassis and bodywork manufacturers and all suppliers were doubtless keen to land an order with GCT. However, after several inspections, the contracts were placed for fourteen buses at a cost of £17,000. The Tramways Committee recommended that seven manufacturers would each supply two chassis. They were:- John I. Thornycroft & Co Ltd; Halleys Industrial Motors Ltd; Bristol Tramways and Carriage Co Ltd; Leyland Motors Ltd; Norfolk Motor and Coach Works (Commer Car); Peric Motor Co. Ltd. (AEC); and D. Carlaugh (sic) & Sons (Tilling-Stevens). The bodies were to be built to the Committee's specifications by:- F. D. Cowieson (4); R. Mitchell and Sons (2); Norfolk Motor and Coach Works (2); and Wm. Law and Sons (2). Tilling-Stevens was to supply its own bodies as would the Peric Motor Company. All were specified as 30-

seaters featuring rear entrance and front exit. The bodies would be divided into smoking and non-smoking compartments. While the contemporary trams retained wooden seating, these pioneer buses were doubtless given leather upholstery to cushion the effects of hammer blows from the solid tyres on cobbled streets.

By May 1924, it was obvious that delivery could not meet the deadline for the track renewal programme and the Department had to hire buses from Scottish General Transport. Later that month, some changes in the initial orders were made when F. D. Cowieson was asked to provide two further bodies for the Tilling-Stevens chassis at a cost of £415 each. Petrol-electric transmission was standard on this make at the time. Incidentally, bodywork — often quoted as 'AEC' for buses numbered 5 and 6 — would likely to have been manufactured by Short Brothers or Strachan & Brown. These firms supplied AEC with many early vehicles as the chassis manufacturer concentrated on the latter aspect of motorbus construction.

The first of the trial buses had been delivered by late August, yet no decision had been made as to their employment. In November, the 23rd Scottish Motor Show was held in Glasgow just as the local Albion Motor Car Company was celebrating its Silver

Although Glasgow's inaugural buses of 1924 had bodywork to a uniform specification, each incorporated detail differences reflecting different manufacturers' variations in interpretation. The cost per bus ranged from £775 for the Halleys up to £1,054 for the Tilling-Stevens, the latter doubtless influenced by their electric transmission. In this scene No. 8 (a Leyland GH6) and No. 10 (a Tilling-Stevens TS3AX) are shown. Both had bodywork by Cowieson, to remain an important supplier to the fleet until the late 'thirties.

Jubilee; it did not miss the chance to stress the lack of any orders from GCT!

At last a use was found for the buses. From 8th December 1924, a six-minute service using twelve of the 'cars' would operate between Greendyke Street (near Glasgow Green) and Maryhill (LMS Station), via Clydeside and Partick, keeping well off the tram lines! The buses were stabled at Parkhead Depot, which was situated near the eastern end of the route. The service seemed to have been a success from the passengers' point of view by all accounts — except financial, because a deficit of over £5,000 had accrued in the first year. The only change to the fleet in that first year was the conversion of the solid tyres to pneumatic ones which had gained considerable popularity and helped to match the smooth-running tramcars. In 1925, however, time was fully committed to planning experiments before embarking on the modernisation of the tram fleet, the need for which was clearly appreciated.

Private operators were beginning to make inroads into Glasgow municipal transport's cash bags; nevertheless, it was the Department's own motorbuses that replaced the single deck tram (92) which plied along Stobcross Street, linking the river ferry with Finnieston, on a 'pay as you enter' basis. Two years later, in 1927, the bus service was withdrawn also. Trials were continuing with other makes of buses during this period and a double-decker AEC 504 bus with a Birmingham Corporation-style body built by Short Brothers, Rochester (registered GB 6914) was put in service until December 1925, when it

The side view of one of the original fleet of single-deckers shows the high saloon floor, with four steps, unavoidable on the straight-framed goods-style chassis of the day. This example has a Halley chassis of the 40 hp P series, which, unusually for that date, had a six-cylinder engine, and bodywork by Law.

The two pairs of Leyland Lion buses delivered in 1927 marked a considerable advance on the original fleet of three years earlier. Pneumatic tyres and forward-control layout were obvious changes, but this original Lion model was also quite a lively and smooth-running bus. The floor level had come down significantly, though Glasgow was one of a number of municipalities to favour the optional high-roof version of the Leyland-built body. They were on PLSC1 chassis and seated 29 with the two-door body layout still favoured — the rear-end design, with cut-away entrance, was of a style quite widely favoured in Scotland though occasionally also found elsewhere. Almost identical buses had been supplied to Edinburgh in 1926 and to Dundee in 1927. Seen at Leyland before delivery is 17. The black-edged silver fleetname lettering was to remain characteristic of GCT buses until 1943.

was sent to Sheffield Corporation and became its No. 106 in February 1926. It also demonstrated for other operators including Sussex Motors Ltd, an unsuccessful aspirant to operation in Brighton, possibly before delivery to Glasgow, in February 1925.

Nearer home, some councillors expressed the belief that Glasgow Corporation had failed in its duty to provide services to new housing estates which were being built around the city,

and private operators had moved in to cream off the traffic. This resulted in continual attrition between GCT, the Police, Magistrates and private owners which continued until 1930 when the Road Traffic Act of that year effectively gave the Corporation a monopoly of road passenger transport inside the (then) city boundary.

A further cautious expansion of the bus fleet occurred when four additional single-deck buses materialised in 1927

in the form of Leyland Lions. Numbers 15 and 16 arrived in February with 17 and 18 delivered in July. In between came the first Albions, two of the PM28 type with Cowieson bodies (19 and 20). Perhaps Albion's earlier protests had paid dividends! Councillors once again expressed their alarm at the dramatic increase in 'pirate' buses stating that 'Purchases will have to be made if the Corporation is not to be forced into hiring buses to carry the residents of

Albion was an obvious choice of chassis for a city whose council was always conscious of pressure to support local industry. Two of the PM28 type delivered in 1927 were followed by ten more in 1928, all having Cowieson bodywork. 25 and 26 of the latter are seen on test, climbing Gardner Street, Partick. The forward-control versions of this series of 30/60 hp models retained the radiator position over the front axle as used on the normal-control type, giving an appearance which soon made them seem dated. As with the Lion buses, the original two-door layout was later altered to one with rear entrance only. The two vehicles are pictured again on the hairpin bend at Strathblane on page 15.

A newly delivered Leyland Titan upstages a retreating 'white' open balcony standard tramcar at Charing Cross in 1928. Commercial postcard publishers were always anxious to display the latest vehicles in their street scenes so that they would not become dated.

Knightswood, Mosspark, Kelvindale and Carntyne—as tram extensions to these places are out of the question due to the cost'. And purchase they certainly did! Ten Albion single-deck buses with Metcalfe bodies and fifteen Leyland Titan double-deckers were ordered. The 'Buy Glasgow' faction was at work again and in January 1928, Cowieson was awarded the contract to build the single-deck buses—they duly arrived two months later with fleet Nos. 21-30. These were to be the last single-deckers purchased until 1939. The 1927 buses 15-20 were delivered with dual entrance/exit doorways and it is interesting to relate that their two-door layout was no more successful than the variations on this theme in the 'fifties, 'sixties and 'seventies which were inevitably rebuilt with one single entrance/exit. The Leyland Lions and two Albions had their front doors out of use and removed by 1930. Additional seating for two people was incorporated with a single rear doorway.

When Leyland Motors introduced its revolutionary Titan chassis at the 1927 Motor Show, the Company could hardly have envisaged that forty years later the Titan would still be in production, albeit

redesigned so completely as to have little but the basic concept inherited from the original. Until 1928, double-deck motorbuses tended to be tall ungainly vehicles, their use being mainly confined to large cities, where double-deck trams were familiar and considered (and proven) safe to the travelling public.

The Titan introduced a chassis on which a double-deck body could be fitted, but with an overall height of around 12ft. 10in.; the Titan was at least 2ft. lower than conventional double-deck trams or buses and could be used under many bridges which were previously barred to double-deckers.

The pneumatic tyres and enclosed top deck gave the bus its characteristic 'modern' look and with a smooth-running and reliable petrol engine it was set to take the bus industry by storm. On 10th February 1928, Glasgow Corporation's first Leyland Titan entered service, and by June all fifteen had been delivered (51-65). They were to be the standard Titan specification, with lowbridge open-stair bodies, seating 24 downstairs and 27 upstairs, incorporating a sunken gangway and four-abreast seating. The buses soon

proved popular and in August the Tramways Department, obviously impressed, placed an order with Leyland Motors for 100 buses to be delivered by December. This was the largest single order yet placed for the Titan, probably the largest single order for any 'provincial' road transport vehicle, and it is most unlikely that Leyland could have carried out this order on its own in the time available. Therefore, a portion was sub-contracted to other body-builders, leaving Leyland to produce the chassis. By November, 42 were still to be delivered.

Every two years, the Scottish Motor Show was held at Glasgow's Kelvin Hall and in 1928, the Leyland Titan was one of the star exhibits. One was displayed, not with Leyland bodywork, but with a locally-built Cowieson body. It carried No. 142, and Cowieson proudly claimed to have built 30 double-deck buses for Glasgow 'to Leyland specification'.

In the technical press at this time, an advert appeared for Short Brothers, better known for building bodies for AEC chassis. They had recently completed 27 buses for GCT and included a photograph. Close examination of this vehicle featured in the advert leads to

the belief that the 'piano-front', so characteristic of Leyland-bodied Titans, may have been less pronounced than the Lancashire product. With documentary evidence lacking and, even less, photographic proof, it is not possible to state the exact fleet number for each make of body (except 142). What is certainly known is that the buses were not delivered in an orderly fashion. By January 1929, things had become very complicated and a summary of the events of that year make matters clearer. It should be remembered that, by September 1929, Leyland had introduced a closed-stair body and also a 'normal-height' body, giving more options for its many customers — as well as headaches for the transport historian! A very early example of Leyland's 'Hybridge' body, as the normal-height version was called, was photographed in Glasgow livery (but unnumbered) that same month. It was noteworthy for multiple emergency exits, six in all, and the Corporation appears to have taken a close interest in this subject, then at a formative stage.

From this evidence it can be surmised that 142 was built in advance for its inclusion at the Kelvin Hall and 133-162 had Cowieson bodies to Leyland design. 165 was the 'prototype' closed stair Cowieson lowbridge bus; 163 and 164 followed in June. 172 and 173 were 'prototype' highbridge Cowieson buses, and fifteen of the 174-248 batch had lowbridge bodies, the remainder being highbridge. A word of explanation is necessary to illustrate the differing interpretations of the phrases 'lowbridge' and 'highbridge'. Leyland-designed 'lowbridge' bodies introduced the offset sunken gangway to the upper-deck resulting in four abreast seating. Even by present-day standards, the total height of 12ft. 10in. was remarkable. Cowieson's version of the low-height bus was 13ft. 5in. high with three abreast seating, incorporating a row of single seats on the offside and a passage inbetween. Its highbridge body had conventional 2 x 2 seating with centre gangway upstairs but was still under 14ft. Leyland marketed its highbridge body as 'Hybridge' and was 14ft. in height.

It must not be thought that Leyland had a monopoly on vehicle manufacture in 1929, as the Department was looking at rival makes. G. J. Rackham, the designer of the Leyland Titan, having seen his brainchild take shape, resigned from Leyland Motors to assume a similar position at AEC. The outcome of this move was the introduction in late 1929 of the AEC Regent double-deck chassis. This was strongly reminiscent of the Lancashire product although the wheelbase was shorter. The Regent differed in two important aspects which were immediately noticeable, i.e. it incorporated a much neater radiator and front end, and, because Leyland had patented its low-bridge design with the offside sunken gangway, the AEC Regent had a centre gangway upstairs from the initial production. AEC itself had no body-building factory and therefore outside contractors were used. Nevertheless, the design closely followed the Leyland outline, except for one important feature — the camel hump roof. When viewed from the kerbside, the Regent gave the impression of being as low as the

January 1929:	delivered — 85, 162	open stair, lowbridge Leyland body.
	165	Cowieson closed stair lowbridge.
May 1929:	delivered — 81, 86, 102, 103, 105, 144	open stair, lowbridge Leyland bodies.
June 1929:	delivered — 146, 147, 152, 155-9, 161	open stair, lowbridge Leyland bodies.
	163, 164	Cowieson closed stair, lowbridge bodies.
September 1929:	delivered — 172	Cowieson 51-seat highbridge body.
	173	Cowieson 48-seat highbridge body.
November 1929:	delivered — 166-170	Leyland closed stair, lowbridge bodies.
January 1930:	delivered — 171	Leyland closed stair, lowbridge body.
February 1930:	delivered — 174-188	Cowieson closed stair, lowbridge bodies.
	189-248	Cowieson closed stair, highbridge bodies.

256 was one of a small batch of AEC Regents with Cowieson bodywork delivered in 1930. They were much neater looking at the front of the chassis than their Leyland counterparts. Ten were to enjoy very long lives, albeit latterly with utility bodywork, but 256 was withdrawn in 1943. Remedial treatment, presumably to prevent rain ingress to the front roof dome is evident but the smartly dressed crew standing in front look proud of their almost new charge. Note the offside-front upper-deck emergency door, characteristic of this body design.

A rear view of Regent 250, numerically the first added to the fleet, illustrates well the typical upright rear of a standard GCT Cowieson body of the 1930-31 period. Note the registration number position and that no escape provision exists at the rear of the upper deck, the legal requirement not then being in force, although the platform rear window is also hinged for this purpose. Both vehicles were converted for further use in the service fleet. See page 79.

lowbridge Leyland Titan, but the centre gangway upstairs gave rise to the hump in order to provide adequate headroom. The demonstration model (MT 2114) performed in various parts of the country, including Glasgow, under a veil of secrecy and it appeared at the 1929 Motor Show at Olympia in GCT colours. In October 1929, Glasgow had announced an order for 25 Regents along with 75 Titans, so perhaps AEC could justify the repainting of its demonstrator for this occasion. It certainly made an impression on Halifax Corporation because not only did the Yorkshire town order Regents, but it also adopted Glasgow's livery after seeing MT 2114. This remained Halifax's colour scheme until 1974 (when West Yorkshire PTE took over the town's buses)—a longer period, incidentally, than its precursor!

Delivery of Glasgow's first Regents (250-274) took place in May-June 1930 with the (by now) standard Cowieson body with 24 seats downstairs and 27 above—although they had a single seat at the front offside to allow space for Cowieson's unusual top deck emergency door positioned at the front. Cowieson-bodied Regents had the more conventional well-rounded rather than the 'camel-hump' roof; this latter style was soon to disappear. Also appearing at Olympia were other

makers all eager for sales in the rapidly expanding market. Crossley introduced its Condor chassis with 50-seat Brush body, later registered GE 7974, painted in Glasgow colours and operated by GCT in February 1930. It subsequently became Aberdeen Corporation No. 81, after appearing at the 1930 Scottish Show. Vulcan Motors, Southport, also displayed its latest chassis, the Emperor, alongside the Crossley, with a 51-seat enclosed-stair body. However, only a chassis was at the Kelvin Hall the next year but, evidently impressed by it, the Transport Committee ordered 25 Emperors and also arranged for a short term loan of WM 4829, an Emperor demonstrator. Demonstrating outside the Kelvin Hall was a Daimler CF6 double-decker with a Park Royal body featuring a special emergency exit at the front; it eventually became Dundee Corporation No. 62, after being borrowed by Glasgow.

The Vulcan Emperors arrived in two distinct batches, 350-360 in June 1931 and up to 374 in March 1932, all having Cowieson 48-seat bodies. This delay may have been the result of financial difficulties at the Southport factory, as no sooner had Glasgow's buses been delivered than the company went into liquidation. The vehicles were very short-lived in their original form and, after only three or four years' service,

many had their original radiators and engines replaced by units of Leyland manufacture. It must remain a mystery to this day as to why the Corporation purchased such a strange batch of vehicles, with such an unsatisfactory beginning. By 1940, their demise was in sight, and as no records survive of their subsequent owners (if any), one can only assume that they were scrapped—after only eight years' use. Photographic evidence of their stay in Glasgow is even rarer. More successful, however, were the Titans and the Department found that the 258 TD1s were everything that the Leyland adverts claimed. After an accident in 1935, the chassis of Titan 99 was incorporated into a tow wagon, whilst its body was placed on the chassis of Regent 266. Thus the fleet gained the only open-staired AEC to operate in the city! A year later, a similar move placed the body from 144 onto the chassis of 226 and formed a very late open-staired Leyland. Number 188 was an earlier victim to be rebodied in 1932 by the firm of Hurst Nelson, Motherwell, who had supplied 30 tramcar bodies for Glasgow some four years previously. This solitary body from the Lanarkshire firm incorporated a novel emergency escape ladder from the top deck.

Two vehicles which have still to be mentioned both came from AEC at

Parkhead, Glasgow's first bus garage, in the early 'thirties. Most of the buses visible in the foreground are Leyland Titan TD1 models with Cowieson bodywork, Glasgow's standard combination of the 1930-31 period, when many such buses were added to the fleet. 203, on the left, is of this type, whilst 373, at the edge of the picture, was one of the 25 Vulcan Emperor buses with similar bodywork.

Southall. The first (249) was an AEC Regent delivered in July 1931, and was an early example of a diesel-engined Regent, probably to test operating results alongside its petrol-engined brothers. Diesel engines were much heavier than petrol ones and this presumably accounts for the loss of four seats from the standard double-decker capacity in an effort to keep the maximum laden weight within the then limits. By March 1934, it was reseated to 51; the diesel was replaced by a petrol engine around 1935-36, finally reverting to oil by 1938.

Backtracking slightly to the 1929 period, at the same time as AEC introduced its Regent double-decker, a six-wheeled version called the Renown was also launched. With a wheelbase of 16ft. 6in., the 663-type bus chassis were mainly purchased by operators who required higher seating capacities than was legally possible within the confines of a 25ft.-long four-wheeler. Over three-quarters of the Renowns built were

operated by London General Omnibus Company. However, three 663-model chassis were assigned for elsewhere. The first was a demonstrator destined for and eventually operated by Birmingham Corporation (92). The third was the chassis exhibited at the 1931 Olympia Show, and in between came the chassis which eventually became Glasgow No. 50. Fitted with a Cowieson body seating 60, it was delivered in September 1931, and having been used as a demonstrator, bought by GCT in 1932 and numbered 50. In 1935 when the new Albions were due (1-50), the Renown was renumbered 238. Three years previously, the original 238 had suffered an accident which proved to be 'fatal'. The chassis became a lorry and the body was placed on the chassis of 313. Of the few photographs available, none show the Renown carrying any fleet number (apart from a view taken after its withdrawal). Its longevity enabled it to acquire a cream roof. (*Chapter 15*).

As well as being a period of great economic depression, the early 'thirties were, paradoxically, times of great expansion as far as public transport was concerned. Many rival firms vied for the lucrative tramcar replacement orders being offered by municipalities and companies alike, while they also catered for the expanding motor bus fleets as towns outgrew their boundaries and the population became more mobile. Glasgow had its barrage of demonstrators and trials and an examination of the fleet strength published in *Commercial Motor* in 1933 reveals several buses which, while never owned, warranted inclusion in the figures. With hindsight, they can be identified as follows:-

'1 Leyland x 60 seat double decker' —
   Leyland Titanic (rival to the six-wheeled Renown) with Cowieson body, later to become Sheffield Corporation 111 (WE 7039).

The 25 Vulcan Emperor double-deckers of 1931-32 had similar Cowieson bodywork to their Leyland and AEC contemporaries but were much less successful. The Glasgow order was the largest placed for this short-lived model but, with the Southport-based concern in receivership, coping with the model's shortcomings was made more difficult and the vehicles seem to have seen little use after about 1938.

'1 Albion x 60 seat double decker' —
> Albion Valorous, another 6-wheeler which, after being used as a demonstrator, was bought by Young's Bus Service, Paisley and became their No. 71 (GG 9461) in 1933.

'1 Albion x 51 seat double decker' —
> A prototype Albion Venturer (GG 8742), later to become Young's No. 72, also in 1933.

One bus that was clearly intended to win orders from Glasgow was a 1932 Bristol G-type (HY 6605) with 51-seat Cowieson body, finished in GCT livery, and probably inspected by the Department, although never appearing in any fleet survey. It became Bristol Omnibus Company No. C3003, and Glasgow never purchased any Bristol vehicles until much later in our story. One puzzling feature of these fleet details from 1932-35 was the mention of six or seven Leylands (TD1s) with 50-seat bodies, which must remain unexplained. Were they early diesel conversions?

All the vehicles purchased in the first ten years had either been sold to other operators, converted into service vehicles, or scrapped by the Department by 1945, with very few exceptions. However, many of the Titans were used by other operators for some time after disposal by GCT. While it is impossible to relate here each individual vehicle's subsequent history very accurately, several disposals to better-known fleets

around 1940 are worth mentioning. Young's Bus Services, Paisley received Titans 72, 84, 90, 130, 131 in 1940 and later 81, 178, 179, 181-4, 190, 208, 222, 225, 230, 284, 291, 299. Garner's, Bridge of Weir bought 133, 167 and 169 as well as hiring 212 and 285. Graham's of Paisley took 209, 242, 286, 296. W. Alexander & Sons (Falkirk) received 176, 197, 201, 207, 213, 215, 216, 229, 231, 244, 245, 247, 248, 275, 321, 324, 329, 334, 335, 337, 343. Caledonian Omnibus Co Ltd purchased 119, 123, 137, 149, 152, 153, 159, 203, 220, 281 and at least six of these buses survived until this Tilling Group company was taken over by Western SMT in 1950.

In November 1938, the Department investigated the possibility of using redundant double-deckers as mobile libraries to visit outlying areas. Each conversion was estimated to cost around £1200 with adults' books on the lower deck and juveniles' above! Titan 92 was converted in 1939 for this purpose. Number 70 was used by Glasgow Corporation Welfare Department while 150 became a mobile GCT canteen. Tow wagons were built from the remains of 250, 258, 259 and 330. Many years later, part of the chassis of 72 was rebuilt and formed the basis of a preserved Keighley-West Yorkshire bus No. K451. A large number of TD1s were converted into ambulances and civil defence vehicles for use during the 1939-45 war. They are indicated in the notes below.

The AEC Renown carried a 'stretched' version of the Glasgow standard Cowieson bodywork, completely to the Corporation's specification. Even by 1933, the bus carried no fleet number. In typical AEC fashion for the period, it had been built in 1931 as a demonstrator, together with a similar chassis for the Birmingham fleet, and then supplied on extended loan before being taken into stock by GCT. Note the course being adopted by the Armstrong-Siddeley tourer driver — caution was sometimes needed in crossing tram tracks at a fine angle with the narrow section tyres of those days.

The next chapter will reveal which firms were chosen to supply further GCT orders after several demonstrators had been inspected. The motorbus was here to stay after its late and shaky appearance. Leyland and AEC were in a strong position for orders but a newcomer was to make an entrance into the fleet, as well as the local Albion company.

The first fourteen buses were registered GB 6900-13 in ascending order, being two each of Commer 45 hp, Halley 40 hp, AEC 401, Leyland GH7, Tilling-Stevens TS3AX, Bristol 4-ton and Thornycroft J chassis. Cowieson provided the bodies for 7-10, 13 and 14, whilst the remainder were supplied by Norfolk (1 and 2), Law (3 and 4), 'AEC' (5 and 6) and Mitchell (11 and 12). They were all sold by 1929 except 2 which was retained as a 'learner' until 1939 and then a civil defence vehicle.

The Leyland Lions had registrations GD 5324-5, GD 7574-5, and were PLSC1 models with Leyland bodies. All sold by 1934.

Albions 19-20 were GD 7558-9 while 21-30 were GD 9716-25.

Titans 51-65 were registered GD 9701-15, 66-165 were GD 2401-2500, 166-242 were GE 7200-7205, 6717, 6785, 7206-7274 respectively. 243-8 were GG 631-6.

AECs 250-274 had type 661 chassis and 250-267 were registered GE 7282-99, whilst 268-274 were GE 7275-81. The 1930 batch of Titans were 275-349: GG 901-50, 2101-25 respectively. Oil-engined AEC Regent 249 had a 661 chassis being registered GG 4034 and the Renown 663-type 50 (later 238) was registered GG 4681.

The Vulcans were registered GG 2126-50.

The following buses were used as (c) Civil Defence, (m) on Hire to London Transport 1940-41 or (w) works vehicle:-

(c) 52-4, 59, 61, 64, 69-71, 73, 76-8, 80, 82-3, 87, 89, 94-5, 97-8, 101-2, 104-7, 111-3, 115, 117-8, 121-2, 126, 128-9, 132, 134-6, 138-9, 142-3, 146, 151, 156.

(m) 177, 188, 191, 195-8, 201, 205-11, 213, 221, 227-8, 231, 234, 247, 278, 281-2, 288-90, 293, 296, 318, 320, 343-4.

(w) 4, 7-8, 150, 238, 250, 256, 258-9, 330.

Glasgow Corporation's trams, of which there were then over 1,100, still outnumbered its buses by about two to one in 1938, the year when the Empire Exhibition was held in the city. The dominance of the tram is even more marked in this scene in Renfield Street, though at least the buses, including Leyland Titans 143, one of the 1928 batch, and 470, a 1937 TD5 with Cowieson body, did not find parked cars obstructing their progress. The anti-tram lobby was becoming vociferous about the congestion, a precursor of that experienced under deregulation of buses nearly 40 years later. The final series of service numbers had just been introduced on the trams, most of those visible being 'Standards' though a 'Coronation' is visible second in line beyond the junction. Note the Glasgow office of Illife, then publishers of *The Autocar*, *Motor Transport* and *Bus and Coach*.

Chapter two: The standard bus evolves

By 1934, none of the original 30 single-deckers survived in passenger service in Glasgow and the large influx of double-deckers had ensured that single-deckers would play little part in the expanding network of routes for the time being. The Department was then ready to place large orders for the motorbus fleet but the question remained — which vehicles would be most suitable for Glasgow? We have seen in the previous chapter that trials had taken place with other makes apart from AEC and Leyland.

In 1933 Albion Motors introduced a double-deck chassis named Venturer and an example with 51-seat Cowieson body was previewed at the Kelvin Hall in Glasgow in 1932 and a year later at Olympia. Halley's Motors, a rival firm to Albion, expressed concern at Glasgow

Corporation purchasing large numbers of English vehicles. As long as it continued to do so, they felt that there was little prospect of any local manufacturers getting any orders. Halley hoped to introduce a new double-decker in 1934, and obviously looked towards GCT for orders. Albion had a well-timed ace to play. In March 1934 Glasgow was treated to a procession through the city of vehicles ranging from 1901-1933 by way of celebrating the recent warrant of appointment by His Majesty the King. When the Department made it known that 110 oil-engined buses would be required, offers were made by almost every manufacturer. To ensure fair play, the Lord Provost and a Bailie opened the tenders and they were examined by

experts before any decision was made.

In April 1932, a 6-ton Leyland Bull lorry had been fitted with a Beardmore diesel engine for trials in Manchester. Beardmore had long been an established Glasgow manufacturer of heavy machinery but, after the depression in 1929-30, diversified their interests and produced diesels (or 'heavy oil engines' as they were then known) for rail-coaches and buses. One of GCT's Leyland Titans, 318, was fitted for a trial period. Although GCT ordered 30 Beardmore engines for use in new Albion buses, the Dalmuir factory subsequently ceased production of engines as they had proved not to be reliable. The Corporation, however, played safe by inaugurating an experiment in 1934 using ten Leyland 6-

There was a gap of several years between the last of the 'short stay' Vulcans and the appearance of a new breed. Cowieson bodywork was chosen again for 50 new Albion Venturer double-deckers with fleet numbers beginning at 1 again in 1935. The first is seen (right) at the Kelvin Exhibition Hall, on the Transport Department's stand. The first 20 had Gardner 6LW engines but the remainder, originally with Beardmore units, were of similar appearance, entering service in 1936. Alongside is Horse tram 543, forty years older than the bus, but still surviving today in the very same building!

cylinder 8.0-litre oil engines.

In addition, a Leyland Titan demonstrator, TJ 3278, visited the city, apparently soon after being built in 1934. It was an example of the then current TD3c variant, the c signifying its torque convertor transmission, an early approach to today's automatic systems, sold under the name 'Gearless'.

In December 1934, it was finally revealed which companies had been selected to supply the Department with new vehicles. Leyland Motors would supply 60 Titan TD4c chassis, while Albion would manufacture 50 Venturer chassis. It was not stated who would body the Leylands, although it would probably have been Leyland themselves, but most definitely the Albions were to have Cowieson bodies. The National Union of Vehicle Builders (NUVB) raised objections to the order. Their argument was that over 500 craftsmen were unemployed in Scotland, and to order English-made bodies was no help at all. After considering the matter, the Corporation revised their plans and all 110 buses were built at Cowieson's factory at St. Rollox, at a £4,000 increase in costs.

Fleet numbers reverted to 1 to accommodate the Albions 1-50, with the Titans following on from 374 (375-434). Albion at this time offered as standard the Gardner 6LW engine for its vehicles. 1-20 were fitted with this unit while, as already mentioned, 21-50 had Beardmore engines. The Gearless

transmission eliminated clutch operation and called for only one movement of the 'gear' lever to engage direct top in the Leyland TD4c buses was supplied, making life much easier for the driver and the passengers! Like most operators of these buses, GCT found this form of transmission rather costly to operate and maintain and so during the war, conventional clutches and gearboxes of AEC manufacture were fitted to several buses.

In August 1936, General Manager James N. Wilson reported to his committee that 75% of vehicles manufactured in the last year had been diesel powered and he was of the opinion that 175 buses should be converted from petrol fuel at a cost of £350 per bus. It was estimated that £4.10/- (£4.50) could be saved per week per bus. Leyland would supply Leyland engines for the Leyland vehicles and AEC would provide their engines for the Regents.

No further vehicles were delivered at that stage but, as the city prepared for the Empire Exhibition to be held at Bellahouston Park in 1938, a large influx of visitors was anticipated. To convey them to and from Bellahouston, a fleet of Coronation tramcars was to be introduced and, to complement them, one hundred buses were ordered in January 1937. This called for 50 Leyland Titan TD5, 25 Daimler COG6 and 25 AEC Regents, with bodies by Cowieson (50) and MCW (50), the latter being

built by Weymann. Again the NUVB complained about the order going south, but this time the Corporation did not agree and stood its ground. It was stated that the cost of these vehicles would amount to £180,000, £30,000 more than the 1935-36 deliveries. A supplementary order was placed with Leyland for 25 oil engines (to replace the Vulcan power units). A new overhaul works was to be constructed at Larkfield.

The vehicles were numbered 435-459 (AEC), 460-509 (Leyland) and 510-534 (Daimler), with the last-mentioned providing the first preselective gearboxes in the fleet. The COG6 chassis incorporated the Gardner 6LW six-cylinder engine as already used in the 1935 Albion buses 1-20. The other makes incorporated 'crash' gearboxes. The bodies were of the conventional rear platform layout with 56 seats; this was to remain standard until 1954 when seating capacities gradually increased before a change to forward entrances in 1960. GCT provided the basic specification and each bodybuilder was free to interpret its own ideas based on a general arrangement drawing prepared in the drawing office at 46 Bath Street. This resulted in the standard Glasgow bus acquiring a family look with detailed differences between manufacturers and from one year's delivery to the next. A streamlined livery was applied to the 1937 and 1938 buses when new, based on the arrangement introduced on the

The lobbying for local unemployment relief resulted in the 1935 batch of Leyland Titan 'Gearless' TD4c models being bodied by F. D. Cowieson, following closely on the earlier batch of 20 on Albion chassis. The all-metal bodies had much softer lines than on the earlier 'frowning' TD1s and AECs and many survived until the late 1940s, long outlasting their Albion-based cousins. Even in those days of 'Automatic Transmission', a starting handle was provided...... for the Supermen of the Department! Note the outswept skirt panels, rare on a double-decker at that date.

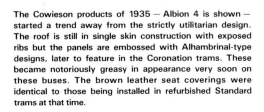

The Cowieson products of 1935 — Albion 4 is shown — started a trend away from the strictly utilitarian design. The roof is still in single skin construction with exposed ribs but the panels are embossed with Alhambrinal-type designs, later to feature in the Coronation trams. These became notoriously greasy in appearance very soon on these buses. The brown leather seat coverings were identical to those being installed in refurbished Standard trams at that time.

Daimler was selected to provide 25 of its Gardner 6LW-engined COG6 chassis for the 1937 intake. These had Weymann bodywork, the chassis type making necessary a floating dash panel, also found on Albion buses both pre- and post-war. Croft-bodied Albion B92 on the left is newly into service in this 1949 picture, showing its original gloss green roof. In its preserved form this has been repainted into the soon-to-be-standard cream. The Daimler 516 already displays this, although withdrawn two years later.

Glasgow Corporation usually extracted the full life span from its vehicles (at least when the engine was located at the front end!) Occasionally some would be sold for further service, witness this view of Pickering-bodied 1939 Albion Valkyrie 692 which left the fleet in 1955 to retire to Dunoon, Argyllshire.

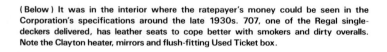

Weymann was chosen for the 30 single-deck bodies built in 1940 on Regal chassis (some of which never entered the fleet) and could readily be distinguished from Albions 686-692 by the lack of vents on either side of the destination display. 711 is seen on a most unusual working on service 38 to Hamiltonhill at the top of Renfield Street. By 1956, half-cab single deckers were fast becoming obsolete and even the conservative Western SMT had underfloor-engined Guys in service as can just be seen, though the vehicle at the left of the picture was a Leyland PS1 of 1949.

(Below) It was in the interior where the ratepayer's money could be seen in the Corporation's specifications around the late 1930s. 707, one of the Regal single-deckers delivered, has leather seats to cope better with smokers and dirty overalls. Note the Clayton heater, mirrors and flush-fitting Used Ticket box.

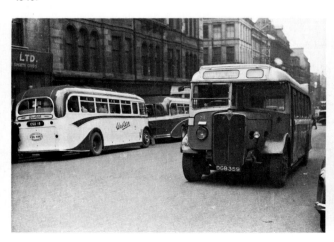

Coronation trams, and very much in vogue with British operators at that time.

By September 1937, the Corporation expressed its unease that only 25 new buses had been delivered—the delay was explained by 'a lack of steel'. By the New Year, all except 520 and 522-534 had arrived and even these remaining Daimlers reached Glasgow by March.

To ensure a continuity of deliveries, a further 100 buses were ordered in February and the steel difficulties appear to have been resolved. Regents remained a popular choice—85 were ordered along with fifteen Venturers from Albion, of a new CX19 type, which offered the newly-introduced Albion 9.08-litre engine as a power unit. Bodywork was again split between manufacturers, with Weymann supplying 50 bodies and Cowieson providing the remainder, being numbered 535-599—AEC/Weymann, 600-619—AEC/Cowieson and 620-634—Albion/Cowieson. Albion chose No. 634 to represent the newly-introduced CX19 model at the 1938 Kelvin Hall Motor Show and it had sliding railway-type windows fitted instead of half-drop ones. Ironically, this appears to have been Cowieson's last bus body; certainly its last for Glasgow Corporation. Investigation into the firm has revealed little due to the passage of time, but the Charles Street factory was still extant until 1953, although as far as is known, no bodies were produced during or after World War II. Although Cowieson was a manufacturer of temporary offices before the first War (Edwardian Portakabins!) and first supplied Edinburgh Corporation with single-deck bodies in 1920-21, its largest customer was undoubtedly GCT.

All these 1938 buses were soon in service to cope with the additional passengers for the Empire Exhibition, some being used on special services introduced during the summer from various districts to Bellahouston Park.

Glasgow's standard pre-war bus, which we can consider ranging from 435-685 and 724-823, had now developed into a comfortable, well-appointed vehicle, remarkable advances having taken place in the ten years since Titan No. 51 had entered service. The respective chassis manufacturers had improved their products within the contemporary regulations regarding width and length (7ft. 6in. x 26ft.), and incorporated the latest in vehicle design. Taking the Weymann bodies as representative of the pre-war fleet, passengers could expect seats with Dunlopillo cushions downstairs, spring cases upstairs, with chromium top rails and tubular seat frames. Ceilings were painted white upstairs but Alhambrinal covered in the lower saloon, the floor of which was slightly recessed to provide additional headroom. A Clayton DeWandre heater was fitted on the top deck bulkhead, with Anemostat or Ashanco vents providing a change of air. There were 26 seats downstairs and 30 above, with a conventional curved staircase and platform area. Modern lighting made evening travel more pleasant. Bulkhead mirrors and polished wood strapping finished off the interior decor. Externally, the buses were fitted with semaphore direction indicators, extra grab rails on the platform for passengers alighting or boarding and a comprehensive destination screen layout, both front and rear with an additional number screen above the platform.

To emphasise the difference between batches, ranging from 1937-1942 deliveries, the main feature that distinguished each manufacturer's products were as follows:-

(a) **Destination equipment.** Number screen, ultimate destination and 'via' screen in separate apertures:- 375-434, 435-484, 535-599, 600-634, 635.
Number screen and destination/via screens in combined aperture but blacked off between screens:- 485-534.
Number screen and destination/via on one screen:- 636-685, 723-823.
Of the rear displays, 485-534 were fitted with flush mounted, ie, intruded into stairwell; remainder bulged outwards. Rear screens were painted over from 1939-46, and some were removed completely.

(b) **Interior lighting.** 485-599 had roof top mounted lamps in opal shades (round) which were removed during the war.
636-665 had similar lamps but with rectangular shades, also removed during the war. Cowieson bodies had circular globes with the bulbs protruding. 723-823 had exposed bulbs, located above the windows.

(c) **Ventilation arrangements:-** No Cowieson bodies had hopper vents on front upstairs windows. 636-685, 723-823, however, were so fitted but these were sealed up after the war and removed on some buses.
804-823 had slotted vents on each side of destination display and each of the five main side windows per deck had sliding vents. 810 was rebuilt (1950s) with alternate windows sealed and rubber mounted glazing.
724-791 had sliding side vents, others half-drop. Some Cowieson bodies had geared wind-up windows (RT-style). Many half-drop windows were replaced after

The largest batch of immediate pre-war buses were the AEC Regents with Weymann metal-framed bodies — 65 were delivered in time for the Empire Exhibition of 1938. The City Chambers provides an impressive backcloth for 598, temporarily out of service only a stone's throw from the 6 which, fifty years on, still travels along the streets mentioned on the via screen. Weymann had begun building bodywork of similar outline for the South Wales fleet in 1936, but the Glasgow version, seen first on Daimler and Leyland chassis in 1937, had a distinctive character of its own, given by such features as the destination layout as well as the livery.

the war with sliding vents.

784-791 built at Larkfield to Weymann design had alternate sliding windows and no hopper-type front vents.

(d) **Bonnet arrangements:-** The pre-war arrangement on half-cab buses meant that some way of preventing the movement of the flexibly mounted engine, gearbox and radiator and inevitable flexing of the front of the chassis from affecting the overhung part of the body had to be found. On the Albion CX19 and Daimler chassis, the dash panel was fixed to the chassis and needed a rubber seal around the perimeter of the panel, hence the rather ugly arrangement. On the AEC and Leyland buses, the rubber seal was fitted next to the edge of the radiator and along the nearside cab window, the cab structure supplied on the chassis being designed to be built into the body.

AECs 536 and 578 both featured in AEC adverts at the time, publicity making good use of GCT's appropriate 'BUS' registrations.

Another 'odd-man-out' arrived in September 1938; such vehicles are peppered throughout GCT bus history, and No. 635 was no exception. It was one of two AEC Regents ordered separately that summer, and had a Pickering body, then the only one in the fleet and one, it is suspected, supplied by the Wishaw firm as a 'carrot' for future orders. The other single-vehicle order is thought to have been related to a vehicle intended for the 1939 Commercial Motor Show, described later.

As stated earlier in this chapter, single-deckers did not feature greatly in Glasgow's bus fleet after 1928, but eventually demand for a bus route in Maryhill led GCT to order its first saloon vehicles for ten years. These took the form of Albion Valkyries, which had been introduced in 1938, although the seven CX25s for Glasgow were a special order. Pickering 35-seat bodywork was fitted with a single doorway with sliding door behind the front axle. Ordered in February 1939, 686-692 were delivered in time to start service 24 from Knightswood Garage on 10th November. The short Gairbraid Avenue-Gilshochill route via Lochburn Road was a useful link from a previously unserved area to the main tram routes on Maryhill Road; the canal bridge on Lochburn Road had been an effective barrier against full-size vehicles. Interestingly, twenty years later, the route was diverted off Lochburn Road and on to Sandbank Street, where double-deckers could run, but did not; and, a further 24 years later, the first 'Micro-bus' service (M24) returned to Lochburn Road. Such is progress!

More conventional buses ordered in February 1939 included 25 AEC Regents (636-660) with English Electric bodies for the first ten and Weymann the remainder. Twenty-five Albion Venturers were also ordered but were more interesting in that they were to an 'intermediate' type, referring to their overall height of 14ft. 1in. Both English Electric and Pickering supplied these 'low' height deckers (661-685) to enable the Department to replace the lowbridge Titans on four services where such buses were necessary. Situated at Kilbowie Road (service 9), Titwood Road (4A) and Carntyne Road (13 and 22), the bridges were geographically distant from each other. Full-height vehicles were fitted with a notice in the driver's cab that they could not operate services 4A, 9, 13 and 22. In 1940, service 4A was diverted from the low bridge via Shawmoss Road and Haggs Road. A year later, the Kilbowie Road service was split and the single-deck portion within Clydebank was operated by Knightswood Regals, leaving the remaining routes 13 and 22 to be worked exclusively by Albions 661-685 from Parkhead Garage. This they did until their withdrawal, although it was not unknown for conventional Albions to have their roof ventilators removed unintentionally at Carntyne Road!

The NUVB expressed their concern at this latest order and stated that rather than purchase fifteen English Electric bodies (a make new to the fleet), Cowieson should be given the order. The Corporation stated in March 1939 they were not prepared to pay the extra £960 for the local product.

All the 1939 buses had been received by the end of that year, by which time War had been declared, although it was very much 'carry on as before' during this period called the 'Phoney War'. As if to emphasise this attitude, GCT did just that by ordering two hundred buses in September, and there was also one special London-type Regent. RT1 had entered service with London Transport in July and the manufacturers AEC were anxious that provincial operators should try this revolutionary vehicle. Perhaps this Regent RT (723) was the missing AEC from the previous year? However, it was 1940 before it entered service, having been destined for the 1939 Motor Show which was cancelled. Number 723 had a Weymann body akin to Glasgow's standard bus, rather than the familiar London Transport design, which made its debut on RT1. The rather optimistic order for 200 buses was altered by the time actual contracts were signed, being reduced to 130 buses and made up as follows:-

50 Albion Venturers
50 AEC Regents
30 AEC Regal single-deckers
80 MCW double-deck bodies
30 MCW single-deck bodies
20 Pickering double-deck bodies

In reality, the total order for 130 buses was never completed—GCT was now suffering the effects of wartime restrictions and cancellations which began to bite more severely after the dramatic summer of 1940 which left Britain facing the threat of invasion. All orders by this time had to be approved by the Ministry of War Transport and nine of the single-deckers were diverted to other uses by the Ministry of Supply. What was actually delivered in 1940 will make things clearer.

724-773 AEC Regents/Weymann (50)

774-783 Albion Venturers CX19/Weymann (10)

693-722 AEC Regals/Weymann (only 21 vehicles from this batch delivered i.e.693/4/6-9, 701-7/9-13/7/9/22)

804-823 Albion Venturers CX19/Pickering (20)

This left 20 Albion chassis and 20 MCW bodies unaccounted for and the fleet numbers 792-803 were never used. Could these numbers have been allocated to ten of the missing vehicles? Those buses that were delivered in 1940 continued with the high standard of interior finish and the only concession made to wartime conditions was the addition of the compulsory headlight masks and alteration to interior lighting. More details of the fortunes of these and subsequent buses follow in the next chapter.

Of the 'real' pre-war fleet, many survived well into the 'fifties until intensive city operation began to take its toll on both bodies and chassis of vehicles which, having had a planned 8-10 year life-span, had been retained much longer due to events outwith the control of GCT! Ninety-six such vehicles were selected to be rebodied after the war and continued to carry Glaswegians for some further years service (see *Chapter 4*). This is perhaps an appropriate time to consider GCT's motorbus fleet in relation to other Corporation Transport departments.

Glasgow had grown from its bone-shaking start in 1924 with fourteen buses to become the third largest Corporation bus fleet in Great Britain in 1939, with 595 buses. Birmingham was first with 1016 (including 78 trolleybuses) and Manchester followed with 863 (including 76 trolleybuses). The Manager in 1939, Mr R. F. Smith, was given special recognition in July 1939 as he (and one other employee) were the only remaining members of staff to have joined the Corporation Tramways staff 45 years earlier when the first municipal horse trams started their journeys in the city!

Such was the position in 1939 when operators began the thankless and frustrating struggle to keep buses and trams on the road during the very difficult times to follow. With a large modern fleet and strong municipal pride and management, GCT's job was easier than most.

(Right) The zenith of F. D. Cowieson's achievement in providing bodywork for GCT was this design. Their products had gradually grown closer to the appearance of the Weymann style and 612, one of the second batch on AEC Regent chassis, is shown, newly delivered, in 1938 with Coronation tram-style streamlining livery. The bodymaker's transfer can be seen immediately in front of the rear wheel mudguard. This bus went on to become AR287 after rebodying and was sold in 1966.

(Below, left) No sign of austerity yet in the 1940 batch of 50 Regents which Weymann built, though these had been ordered in October 1939, when design was still unfettered. Changes to the specification, however, meant sliding windows and additional air intakes from the earlier 1938 deliveries. It was around 1943 before the inscription 'GLASGOW CORPORATION' was abandoned and transferred to small legal lettering above the General Manager's name. Note the ample provision of hand-rails on the platform — GCT were more generous with this feature than regulations required.

(Below, right) 724, after withdrawal in 1955. Compare this view with the bus when new. The front end has been transformed (probably after collision damage) with rubber mounted glazing and incorporating the post-war standard destination layout. The fleet numbers are much smaller than pre-war.

The 1935 intake of buses, all of which had 28 seats on top and 24 below, were Leylands 375-434 (YS 2021-80) and Albions 1-50 (YS 2001-20, 2081-110). 1-20 had SP81 chassis, 21-50 were M81s.

From 1937 all double-deckers were highbridge buses seating 30 above and 26 below. 435-484 were bodied by Cowieson, 485-534 had Weymann bodies and were registered in sequence BGA 1-100. The AEC chassis were O661. 535-634 were registered BUS 101-200 in order except 611 — BUS 178 and 612 — BUS 177. The solitary Pickering-bodied AEC Regent O661 was BYS 763.

1939 deliveries were registered CUS 801-57 (636-92), and the single-deck Albions had CX25-type chassis. Bodybuilders were: 636-645 (English Electric); 646-660 (Weymann); 661-665 (English Electric); 666-692 (Pickering). Of the AEC Regal O662 buses registered DGB 341-70 (693-722), 695, 700, 708, 714-6, 718, 720-1 were not delivered. They had 35-seat forward-entrance bodies. Numbers 723-783 were registered DGB 371-431, 804-823 were DGB 452-471. The following buses were used as (m) on hire to London Transport in 1940-41: (p) producer gas bus 1942-44 or (w) converted to works vehicle:-

(m) 22, 24, 26-7, 29-39, 41, 43, 45-6, 48.
(p) 642, 657, 705, 725, 727-8, 730, 733, 737-40, 744, 746, 754, 757, 762, 764-5, 769-72, 808.
(w) 637, 650, 740.

(Above) 723 was the only provincial RT-type AEC outside London Transport's fleet until after World War II. It had an approximation of the standard LPTB cab design and the RT bonnet assembly married to a near-standard GCT Weymann body. Note the nearside fuel filler cap, another London feature, and rubber wings, the latter also based on the RT outline. For a non-standard bus, it did well to survive all that GCT could impose in 16 years' rigorous service.

(Above right) In September 1937, the Transport Committee considered the question of placing adverts externally on its buses and trams 'providing nothing was done for them to lose their dignity'. However, a year later, the proposal was rejected and the vehicles were to remain unblemished until 1950. This Weymann-bodied Regent was at least ten years old when one of the 'Fifty-Seven Varieties' was added. 750's dignity had suffered somewhat as an examination of the top deck front windows will reveal.

(Centre) 723 may have had a long life in Glasgow, but, by the end, it was 'on its knees'. Note the collapsed rubber mudguards, a common problem with this seemingly practical idea, the missing lower bonnet side, lack of destination indicators and the half-drop window firmly wedged into a parallelogram shape. Perhaps this explains why this bus was the last pre-war vehicle to feature these windows. 723's life terminated with a cracked chassis frame in 1956.

(Below) 'Room for one more on top'. The two 'unfrozen' Leyland TD7 buses of 1942 spent their first twelve years at Elderslie Garage, and, on that garage closing, were transferred to Larkfield. 827 is seen at Pollok shortly before withdrawal in 1958. It continued the pre-war tradition of having the registration plate mounted above dumb-iron level. They were the only examples of Leyland metal-framed bodywork in the fleet.

The Gardner 5LW five-cylinder engine was quite widely used for double-deckers in other fleets despite the limitations of its 85 bhp power output but had been rejected as inadequate for Glasgow's operating schedules. Early 'utility' bus allocations left no choice, however, and seen here is 101, the first of a pair of Daimler CWG5 buses with Massey bodywork delivered in 1943. Wartime timber quality was often poor and this post-war view shows evidence of a major rebuild introducing rubber glazing.

Chapter three: The war years

The previous chapter has somewhat encroached into the period historians label 'wartime'. However, it is necessary to retrace our steps to 1938 to explore the events which influenced Glasgow's buses in the dark years which followed.

In 1938, the risk of war breaking out became stronger and most local authorities made preparations to ensure public transport would continue to function in the event of fuel shortages, blackouts, power failures, etc. Glasgow was fortunate to have, nearby, a supply of shale oil from West Lothian and this safeguarded the supply of fuel when rationing became necessary. Thought was being given, however, to alternative sources and this led the Department to inspect and use a bus converted to operate on anthracite, a form of smokeless fuel. After a trial run between Glasgow and Drymen, Stirlingshire, it entered passenger service on GCT's 5C route (Knightswood–Croftfoot) in October 1938. Resplendent in its Highland livery of red and cream, No. 76, a Gilford HSG — High Speed Gas (ST 9465) single-decker, ran for 23 days. In his report to the Transport Committee on 18th January 1939, Mr Smith noted that

'the bus had performed well but drivers have found it sluggish with poor acceleration. As such it would not be an attractive proposition for city services'.

When war was declared in September 1939, an immediate black-out was imposed and surface transport had to conform to severe lighting restrictions. At first, black paper was gummed to the windows and eventually all headlamps were masked and interior lighting bulbs on the buses were removed and replaced by 'torpedo tube' shaped bulb holders fitted on the ceilings. Windows were covered with netting to prevent injuries in the event of bomb blast and rear destination screens were painted out until 1946 or, in some cases, removed completely. To make the buses more conspicuous at night, their mudguards and platform edges were painted white. Matt green roofs were intended to do the opposite as far as enemy aircraft were concerned!

Services were greatly reduced to save fuel and tyre wear, but, nevertheless, by January 1940 some 180 buses were off the road due to diesel oil shortage. GCT began trials on service 8 between Larkfield Garage and Clarkston using a

single-deck bus with a bag of compressed gas on the roof. A year later, service 9 was used to try out a bus using 6 cwt of anthracite held in a hopper — enough for one day's journey. Two further experiments involved a form of high and low pressure gas. Glasgow's last petrol-engined buses had been either sold or converted to diesel by March 1940.

While running petrol vehicles on producer gas was not without its problems, it was much more difficult with diesel engines, which did not have spark ignition. GCT pioneered the use of producer gas in diesel engines after experiments were carried out initially converting a diesel engine to spark ignition and, more successfully, using a small amount of diesel fuel injected in the normal way to ignite the gas. AEC Regent 559 was sent to the AEC factory in 1940 to be fitted with a rear platform extension which housed the French Bellay system.

To further the use of producer gas, a national scheme for conversions using trailer-mounted gas producers was mounted. These, incidentally, were built by Bristol. Number 559 was

GCT engineers carried out a considerable amount of work on producer gas as an alternative fuel source during World War II. They developed a method of using producer gas in diesel engines — this was adopted afterwards by a number of other undertakings. Some 1¼ million miles were operated by producer gas-powered buses mainly between 1942 and 1944, but owing to its many disadvantages the experiment was abandoned as soon as emergency fuel conditions eased.

Before the more usual trailer operation of producer gas buses, 559, one of the 1938 AEC Regent buses with Weymann bodywork, was chosen ahead of the others to have Bellay producer gas equipment built onto the rear platform. Other photographs dated March 1940 taken at the AEC works suggest that the installation was carried out there. The large fleet numbers and rear destination screens 'in situ' are clues to early wartime involvement. The bus was later converted to trailer operation.

converted to trailer operation later. One English Electric-bodied AEC Regent had its top deck closed off to make room for a gas bag (642). Service 4A (Croftfoot-Govan Cross) was chosen, operating from Larkfield Garage—an inter-suburban route with one nasty drawback—Menock Road hill—scene of many spectacular incidents, depending on the time of year! The 'gasey' buses operated until 1944, spreading to a newly-introduced 32 service, Clarkston-St. Enoch Square (ex 8C) in May 1943. Gas-powered buses ran 1¼ million miles during their two-year stint, and, when the restrictions were lifted, the Department promptly converted the two services back to diesel operation.

Glasgow Corporation Transport had placed 368 buses into its fleet between 1935 and 1939. As was seen previously, a further 200 were ordered, but only 101 entered service. Nevertheless, this gave the Department the opportunity to dispose of the early TD1s and at least 30 were taken in 1940 by the Civil Defence for use as ambulances.

Efforts were made to make better use of the existing fleet, now that Sunday bus services were to be withdrawn, except for shuttle services to the nearest tram terminus. One of the Albion single-deckers, No. 687, had its 35 seats removed in October 1941 and replaced by 29 longitudinal wooden ones, giving greater standing capacity. Number 686 was altered a year later and, by January 1943, all seven had been altered. As previously mentioned, Glasgow's order for 30 AEC Regal single-deckers had not been realised. By May 1940, 24 had been delivered, including three which were not numbered. A further six were acquired by the Ministry of War Transport in July including Nos. 717, 719 and 722. However, 717 and 722 were returned by May 1943 and 719 after October of that year. Four of the remaining Regals, 693, 697, 705 and 710 had their seat layouts altered in a similar fashion to their Albion cousins. In addition, the 1930 AEC Regents 250-274 had an extra seat added by 1940.

To aid London Transport overcome vehicle shortages during the blitz, Glasgow loaned over 50 buses in 1940, including TD1s and those of the 1935 Albions which had had their Beardmore engines replaced by Leyland ones. Most were returned by May 1941, with a few stragglers staying south until February 1942. These buses are shown below. Others were loaned to Stockton Corporation and Garners of Bridge of Weir, Renfrewshire. Whilst in the latter's service, buses from the 375-434 batch were painted in Garners' livery but retained GCT legal lettering. The Glasgow area's own major blitz occurred in 1941. In March of that year, Clydebank and the west of Glasgow was bombed relentlessly for two consecutive nights. Civilian loss of life was enormous and much damage was done to houses, but surprisingly little to the shipyards or the famous Singer factory where munitions were being manufactured. Tram services in Clydebank were severed from the main network for several days and while Glasgow lost only one complete tram due to enemy action, unlike cities such as Sheffield and London, no motorbuses were totally destroyed. Many, however, suffered blast damage and had windows boarded up. A few days after the Clydebank raids GCT service 1 was operated by Central SMT buses with 'Corporation Service' stickers on the windows. Central supplied the drivers

One of the 1930 AEC Regents rebodied by Alexander in 1944, 92, was fitted with the immediate post-war destination screen layout front and rear. As luck would have it, it was captured on film outside Knightswood Garage, where the reserved track on Great Western Road today still awaits a rapid transit system. The highbridge version of the utility Alexander body showed less of its relationship to Leyland designs than the lowbridge version familiar in Scottish company fleets, though the glazing remained similar.

and GCT the conductors. A week later, Glasgow resumed sole working.

The vehicles and service of S. Young of Carmunnock were taken over by GCT in June 1941, the only such acquisition ever made. S. Young operated second-hand Leyland TD1s between the village of Carmunnock and Carlton Place on the south bank of the river Clyde opposite Clyde Street. Two buses were acquired: CM 8731 (ex-Birkenhead Corporation 104) which Young had bought in 1940 along with VX 5859, which had been London Transport TD105. Neither vehicle was used once the Corporation began operating the route which was numbered 31. CM 8731 was converted in October to a mobile office/canteen for the District Commissioner. VX 5859 was sent to Bridge of Weir in December. This arrangement was short lived and, by September 1942, the bus was back, severely damaged in an accident. It was scrapped soon afterwards. The fleet number 826 may have been allocated to this bus as the number had remained vacant.

Incidentally, the Young's service was operated unchanged by GCT until 1955, when the Transport Department's own stops were observed rather than the black and white 'country' bus stops. St. Enoch Square was made the terminal two years later and, even today, the 'Carmunnock' service is still recognisable.

By 1942, large British manufacturers like Daimler, Leyland and AEC had ceased bus building to concentrate on more essential wartime equipment (for example, Leyland produced tanks) and it was obvious that the high demand for public transport would not be satisfied unless the Government released chassis that had been manufactured using existing stocks of parts, etc. These were known as 'unfrozen' chassis and were allocated to operators as seen fit by the Ministry of War Transport, but not always to the most obvious choice. Glasgow obtained two Leyland TD7s with Leyland bodies, No. 827 in March and 828 in July, allocated in this way to the fleet. The make was not unfamiliar to the engineers, but the bodies were the first Leyland-built type since 1930 for GCT. They were finished mainly to Western SMT specification. Albion had not been regarded as a builder of 'unfrozen' chassis, however, and eight chassis were bodied at the bus works, using MCW frames to pre-war standards during 1942. Somewhere, stockpiles of fittings must have come to light! Two other Albion Venturers, 824 and 825, were sent to Wishaw to be bodied by Pickering to the wartime utility pattern and these arrived in May. The next deliveries were of a different breed entirely!

'Unfrozen' buses could only be considered a stop-gap and other measures were necessary if further new vehicles were to be made available. The Government therefore announced that Guy Motors would start production of wartime Arab chassis for the home market. Previous Guy products were of limited appeal, prominent among the few users being Southampton Corporation. The 1936 Guy Arab chassis 'fathered' many features of the wartime marque and the first production chassis was ready for a bodybuilder in the autumn of 1942. The suppliers of bodies for Guy Arabs were mostly well established and experienced and seven were involved in constructing Glasgow's buses. The National Federation of Vehicle Trades produced drawings to the basic specification laid down by the Ministry of Supply and the Ministry for War Transport. Bodybuilders were supposed to adhere to them, but in practice each company interpreted the drawings differently. There were debatable points, and it was possible to distinguish each company's products on closer inspection. The specification called for steel panels, no heaters and a very spartan finish. A Leyland Titan TD7 was bodied by Park Royal and revealed to the press in October 1941 as the first 'Utility' bus. Destined for London Transport (STD 101), it bore many features to be found in pre-war LT buses. Only one destination aperture was permitted (although operators often added others), with two half-drop windows per deck. Add to this front hopper vents, and a distinct lack of curved panels; the utility bus was instantly recognisable.

Glasgow's first four Guy Arab utility buses with Gardner five-cylinder 5LW engines entered service in 1942. Their

Daimler CWA6 of 1944, 114 was sold in 1954 and continued to give good service with the fleet of A1 at Ardrossan. Northern Counties was able to continue using metal framing from components in stock, rather than using wood as specified for Utility bodies. When the supply was exhausted timber was used. The metal framing could account for its longer life. The silver star on the mesh radiator was an embellishment added on the vehicle's arrival in Ayrshire.

Seven attempts were made by Glasgow Corporation to gain powers to construct motorbus bodies from 1922 until 1946, one in 1935 being defeated only by the House of Lords! In 1942, however, eight Albion Venturer CX19 chassis were bodied at Larkfield Bus Works based on framing supplied by Metro-Cammell. Although both Metro-Cammell and Weymann used the same basic structural design, the two firms' products were usually quite distinctive in character until war conditions led to Metro-Cammell producing what were clearly Weymann designed products. After the war, the situation was to be reversed. 787, with headlamps masked, awaits collection. Late in the war, some of the Brush bodies for the 'DUS' — registered Daimlers may also have been assembled, at Larkfield.

By 1951, the GCT bodies were displaying signs of neglect, as indicated in this view of 788. Sad to say, the dent in the front panel and battered mudguard were not untypical of the bus fleet — unlike the much older trams — and this did little to endear what were rather good buses to the long-suffering travelling public.

R. Y. Pickering of Wishaw was a body builder virtually unknown outside Scotland, until the utility period. In 1928, ten Kilmarnock Bogie tramcars had been supplied to GCT, and various bus bodies followed in 1938-40, but the first utility Pickering bodies were built on Albion chassis in 1942 (824 and 825) and Guy Arab models in 1943. Guys 64 and 65, seen at Knightswood Garage, display the extended bonnet and radiator designed to accommodate the Gardner 6LW engine and in this case doing so as well as the stepped cab windows of the Wishaw product. Despite appearances, these, and 483, the Cowieson-bodied Leyland TD5 alongside, saw further service elsewhere, while the Albions 824 and 825 were rebodied by East Lancs for Glasgow.

Brush bodies had the rear top-deck window unglazed, a further sign of wartime austerity. The utility Guys were numbered from 51-69, following on from the 1935 Albions 1-50. The Daimlers started a new group at 101-169, leaving an appropriate gap to place the rebodied AECs — 91-100. In 1943, Transport Vehicles (Daimler) Ltd, whose factory at Coventry had been put out of action by enemy bombing, began production in Wolverhampton of its version of the wartime chassis. Basically similar to the immediate pre-war COG5 chassis, the Daimler wartime design incorporated the pre-war fluid flywheel and preselective gearbox and this, coupled with a flexible engine mounting, brought a more refined vehicle to bus fleets. As if to enforce the austerity measures, however, the first two Daimlers had their rear top-deck windows unglazed and boarded over. Many examples of vehicles with wooden slatted seats could be seen and felt! Numbers 56-58, 60, 103-121, 128-9, 131-134 were so fitted for a time. Glasgow was given permission to obtain deliveries of Daimler and Guy chassis, to be bodied by various firms in 1943 and subsequent years until 1946. The only low height utility bus in the fleet, ie a sunken gangway design, was No. 55 of 1943, all other buses having the normal highbridge layout. The accompanying table makes the deliveries of Glasgow's wartime buses clearer.

Looking the worse for wear is 43, one of the 1936 Albion Venturer M81 buses originally fitted with Beardmore engines but by then converted with Leyland units, helping out hard-pressed London Transport in 1941. Many provincial operators loaned surplus vehicles in the early Blitz years and Glasgow Corporation was not unusual in supplying life-expired or non standard buses but some, like Aberdeen Corporation, sent their latest buses which seems remarkably generous...

Utility Deliveries 1942-1946

Bodies

Year	Brush	NCME	Pickering	Park Royal	Massey	Weymann	Duple	Total
1942	4	-	2	-	-	-	-	6
1943	-	1★	10	-	3	4	-	18
1944	6	6	-	1	-	5	5	23
1945	32	-	-	-	-	-	2	34
1946	7	-	-	-	-	-	2	9
	49	7	12	1	3	9	9	90

★ lowbridge vehicle

Chassis

Year	Guy Arab Mk I (5LW)	Guy Arab Mk I (6LW)	Guy Arab Mk II (5LW)	Guy Arab Mk II (6LW)	Daimler CWA6	Daimler CWD6	Daimler CWG5	Albion Venturer CX19	Total
1942	4	-	-	-	-	-	-	2	6
1943	1	2	1	7	5	-	2	-	18
1944	-	-	-	4	19	-	-	-	23
1945	-	-	-	-	29	5	-	-	34
1946	-	-	-	-	9	-	-	-	9
	5	2	1	11	62	5	2	2	90

Does not include AEC Regents 91-100 which were rebodied buses.

Daimler CWA6 144, bodied by Brush in 1945, shows clearly the 'relaxed' austerity specification which enabled the use of double-curved dome panels, upholstered seats but not yet enlarged destination equipment. This was an official Brush view, with line-up of officials.

In 1943, a revised utility specification was given to bus builders. By this time the rear upper saloon window could be glazed, but conversely upholstered seats gave way to wooden slatted ones. Glasgow, like most operators removed the unglazed windows and wooden seats as soon as convenient. Glasgow continued to withdraw older buses when their lifespan of around fifteen years expired. Ten of the 1930 AEC Regents with Cowieson bodies were selected for rebodying and dispatched to W. Alexander (Coachbuilders) at Stirling. The resulting vehicles 91-100 lasted well into the 'fifties, fine examples of AEC design and GCT ingenuity. They did have moquette-covered seats from new and this was very much a non-standard feature for wartime buses. At the end of 1944 another 'relaxed utility' specification was drawn up which included upholstered seats, more opening windows, half-drop or sliding vents, and less angular corners on the bodies. The Ministry still continued to allocate vehicles until well into 1946 by which time most chassis and body makers were beginning to resume normal output for passenger transport fleets. This accounts for the remaining utility buses going into service in March (161-2) and May 1946 (163-9), almost a year after hostilities in Europe ended.

Utility petrol-engined Bedford single-deckers had been manufactured for those fleets which had need of such vehicles, but GCT, like most municipalities, did not receive any.

The wartime buses had been built under difficult conditions and with poor quality materials used for body-building, this resulted in the chassis outlasting the bodies in many cases. As will be seen later, 30 of the wartime Daimlers, and the Albions 824 and 825, were rebodied, re-numbered and lingered on in the fleet long after their less fortunate brothers had been sold.

(Top) Another wartime bus to see further service was 68, a 1944 Guy Arab II, with 6LW engine and Northern Counties body. Once in the Graham fleet, the utility screen layout was altered to incorporate 'G.B.S.' Graham's No. 40 takes precedence over another Guy, Paton's No. 44, both on hire work for football fans.

(Above) Duple supplied only nine bodies, all on Daimler CWA6 chassis, for GCT during the war years, but these, being comparatively late examples, did not have the wide centre pillar at the front of the top deck. 159, seen here, along with 131 and 157, received the screen layout first incorporated on 'Lightweight' trams 1001-1004.

CM 8731 was a Leyland TD1 with Leyland 48-seat body (lowbridge), VX 5859 had a similar chassis but carried a Dodson 52-seat highbridge body.
784-791 (DGB 432-9) were Albion CX19 chassis with GCT 56-seat bodies on MCCW frames. 824-5, 827-8 were DGB 440-3.
All deliveries from 1942-46 were utility highbridge buses except 55, which was lowbridge with 55 seats.
The Guy buses can be summarised as follows:- Guy Arab Mk 1 with Gardner 5LW engines. 51-6, 58: Arab II with Gardner 6LW engines, 59-69: Mk II with 5LW engine. 57. The bodies were built by, Brush — 51-54: NCME — 55, 67-9: Pickering — 56-65: Park Royal — 66. Registrations: 51-54 (DGB 444-7), 55, 66 (DGG 701-2), 56-65 (DGG 902-11), 67-9 (DUS 424-6).
The 1930 AEC Regents which were rebodied by W. Alexander were GE 7284, 7289, 7293, 7297, 7299, 7275-9 and numbered 91-100 respectively.
The Daimlers were either CWA6 (103-153, 159-169) or CW5G (101-2) or CWD6 (154-8). Bodies were provided by Massey for 101-2, 106: Weymann for 103-5, 107-9, 112-3, 121: Duple for 110-1, 117-9, 159-162: NCME for 114-6: and Brush for 120, 122-158, 163-9. Registrations: DGB 448-51 (101-2, 106, 121): DGB 706-8 (103-5, 7): DGG 710 (108): DGG 912-20 (109, 112-9): DGG 703-5 (168, 110-1): DUS 427-73 (120, 122-67): DGG 921 (169).

Larkfield Bus Works in Wartime

A 1938 AEC Regent with masked headlamps and white-painted mudguards at the new entrance to Larkfield Bus Overhaul Works opened in 1941.

Prior to World War II, each bus in the fleet was sent to Larkfield Garage for 'dock overhaul' after completing 25,000 miles. In this view, the chassis and body of 1935 Albion Venturer 7 have been separated for overhaul.

During the war, Glasgow Corporation Transport Department organised and maintained the city's entire civil defence transport. In addition, 1,200 vehicles were altered to make them suitable for Civil Defence work and 78 new bodies were constructed at Larkfield for vehicles such as ambulances and mobile canteens. Clearly the temptation to give this ambulance converted from a 1932 Austin Twenty six-cylinder model a bus look with a

'destination-box' was too great to be resisted. The Ford mobile canteen dated from 1931 and had previously been operated as a bus in Suffolk, latterly by Naylor of Halesworth until 1940; it was registered RT 7601. Government defence work included the assembly of 101 Army vehicles, maintenance of cranes and vehicles for the Navy and the machining and testing of various engineering components.

Construction of the lower deck of 790, one of eight Albion Venturers bodied at Larkfield in 1942. A finished product is shown on page 25.

Bodywork of the immediate post-war years from W. Alexander bore a remarkable similarity to contemporary Leyland designs, as conveyed in this view of one of 23 Leyland TD4 chassis of 1935 rebodied in 1949. Whilst other rebodied buses had seating for 56, this batch retained the 52-seat capacity of the original Cowieson bodywork, though rearranged with 26 on each deck. All traces of the 'Gearless' transmission had been removed by this time. L21 (originally 425) is seen before delivery.

Chapter four:

The post-war rebuilds

Although the Transport Department ordered some 480 chassis during the period 1946-1949, bodybuilding and chassis manufacture did not approach anything like their pre-war production rates. This inevitably meant long delays in the delivery and commissioning of new vehicles, and, like other transport undertakings, GCT was faced with vehicle shortages as the usage of public transport in Great Britain reached its peak around 1949-50.

Many of the pre-war buses had survived longer than the eight-year 'norm' for his period and, although their chassis were in reasonable condition, many of the composite (ie timber-framed) bodies and some manufacturers' metal-framed products had deteriorated, especially the Cowieson bodies. The Department, therefore, contrived to modernise the pick of the pre-war buses which, it was reckoned, would then be in a position to give further service. Presumably the success of the first rebodying exercise in 1944 (*Chapter 3*) prompted the Department to continue this practice.

The first (and oldest) chassis to be considered were from the batch of Cowieson-bodied Leyland TD4c buses dating from 1935 (375-434).

Twenty-three, a somewhat puzzling number, were selected, their bodies removed and chassis overhauled. An advert in July 1948 stated that 'tenders would be required to supply 'utility type' motorbus bodies to be fitted on 1935 Leyland chassis, which would incorporate existing 'seating and fittings'. According to the *Glasgow Evening News* at that time, the order was to go to Croft (10), Brockhouse (10) and Scottish Aviation (5) (*sic.*), 25 in all. This was most likely a reference to the bodies built on Albions B89-113. However, W. Alexander's tender was successful and the chassis were driven to Stirling to be fitted. In fact, nothing of the original seating and fittings was used although the 26/26 seating layout was retained. Bearing a distinct resemblance to the then current Leyland body design, the 'new' vehicles were numbered L1-23. Interestingly, no further Leyland buses were rebodied although there were 50 which were two years younger than L1-23. Though L22 had been given an AEC engine and gearbox earlier, it reverted to Leyland units on rebodying.

In the late 'forties, many of the larger bodybuilders had more than enough orders to cope with and there was plenty

of scope for smaller (and in some cases local) companies who hitherto had not been active in building public transport vehicles, or perhaps had specialised only in luxury coaches, to obtain orders from previously undreamt of sources. The next chassis to be dealt with were 45 of the 1937-38 AEC Regents, all with Cowieson bodies, and a variety of firms gained these orders in 1950. Fifteen vehicles received W. Alexander (Coachbuilders) bodies. By then this private company had been divorced from the parent operating company which had been nationalised. Ten vehicles went to Prestwick to be bodied by the Scottish Aviation company which had diversified on a limited scale into the psv market two years earlier. This company had also provided five double-deckers for GCT the previous year—on new Albion chassis. A local company, Scottish Commercial, situated in Glasgow's Townhead district, a few hundred yards from Cowieson's premises, was chosen to build ten and as this company had carried out repairs to GCT buses just after the war, the choice was perhaps not surprising. As Scottish Commercial was the local Crossley Motors agent, the bodies were very similar to Glasgow's

The East-end firm of Croft provided particularly stylish bodies for both rebuilt chassis and new models in 1949-50. AR270, based on a 1937 AEC Regent chassis originally numbered 449, passes a City-bound Central SMT Leyland at Whiteinch in 1960. An inspector will have noted the loose bonnet panel!

Bus crews were often changed over (or 'relieved') in Cumbernauld Road at Aitken Street and BR13, an Albion Venturer CX19, is about to return to Parkhead Garage from this location. Its 1952 East Lancs body is six years older than that of L112 behind, but, nevertheless, has successfully concealed the true age of the chassis. This is, of course, before the days of registration suffixes. The Leyland is a 1958 PD2/24 delivery from Coplawhill.

Scottish Aviation was another relatively local bodybuilder to supply on both new and reconditioned chassis. Here AR279, a 1938 AEC Regent rebodied in 1950, is seen with B111, a 1949 Albion Venturer CX37S at Scotstounhill terminus. The AEC-based version had a noticeably better-proportioned cab than the Albion, whose windscreen style seems curiously awkward, contrasting with the styles of other builders on the same chassis or indeed other buses in the fleet.

Crossley-bodied AECs (A21-70). The fourth company to carry out rebodying on AEC chassis was Croft whose factory was situated in Glasgow's Gallowgate. Ten Albion Venturers had been completed there in 1949, and apart from ten bodies for Glasgow's 1937 Regents, Croft was also supplying another Scottish municipal fleet, namely Dundee, which received ten similar vehicles on Daimler chassis the following year. These rebodied AECs AR266-310 were numbered consecutively above the then highest numbered (anticipated) AEC Mark III Regent A265. Other rebodied buses' stock numbers reverted to '1' with the chassis make letter + 'R' as prefixes.

Pickering-bodied Albion chassis from 1939-40 plus the two austerity buses from 1942 (824 and 825) were the next to be called in. However, no local firms were to gain from this order and it was stated in April 1951 that keen competition had enabled the Department to purchase 30 new bodies cheaper than previously from Yorkshire, although it would have liked to have used local manufacturers. East Lancashire Coachbuilders carried out this work at their Bridlington factory in 1952, the buses returning to be numbered BR1-30.

The final spate of rebodying involved the wartime Daimler buses whose poor quality utility bodywork certainly proved to be no match for the robust chassis. Of the 69 Daimler CW series chassis, 30 with AEC engines were selected, and the order was placed in November 1953 again with East Lancashire Coachbuilders, in this instance built at their Blackburn works. The buses returned in 1954 and entered service numbered DR1-30.

This ended the large scale rebodying of older chassis. A total of 138 buses was dealt with, although there is evidence that a further 39 buses were considered for the same treatment in 1953. The delivery of new chassis had certainly been speeded up by then and the need for such measures was not so pressing. Rebodying enabled the Department to retain chassis which had greatly exceeded their expected lifespan, some lasting 25-27 years. They were a great credit to their original designers.

With the recent phasing out of the Bus Grant, payable to operators of stage carriage vehicles, perhaps the rebodying process undertaken so readily in the early 'fifties might make a comeback in the near future!

The original Cowieson bodies on Leyland and AEC chassis; and Pickering and various utility bodies on Albion and Daimler chassis were replaced by W. Alexander; batches (a), (b), (c); Croft (d); Scottish Commercial (e); Scottish Aviation (f); East Lancashire (g), (h), (i). New fleet number is in brackets.
(a) AEC Regent O661. 252 (91), 257 (92), 261 (93), 265 (94), 267 (95), 268 (96), 269 (97), 270 (98), 271 (99), 272 (100).
(b) Leyland TD4cs forming 'L' class. 375 (1), 376 (12), 377 (3), 385 (4), 386 (13), 388 (5), 389 (6), 390 (16), 396 (7), 402 (8), 407 (9), 409 (2), 424 (20), 425 (21), 426 (22), 432 (11), 434 (23), 412 (14), 413 (17), 414 (15), 417 (18), 421 (10), 422 (19).
(c) AEC Regent O661s forming 'AR' class: 435-44 (296-305), 450 (306), 453-4 (307-8), 458-9 (309-10).
(d) 445 (266), 446 (267), 447-9 (268-70), 451 (271), 452 (272), 455-7 (273-5).
(e) 600 (294), 606 (295), 610 (286), 612 (287), 613 (288), 615 (292), 616 (290), 617 (289), 618 (291), 619 (293).
(f) 601-5 (283, 276, 277, 284, 278), 607-9 (279-81), 611 (282), 614 (285).
(g) forming 'BR' class: 666-85 (BR1-20).
(h) 806, 808-9, 811, 813-4, 820-1, 824-5 (BR21-30).
(i) forming 'DR' class: 105-110, 112-3, 116-8, 120, 122-7, 130, 135, 137, 141-2, 144-6, 150, 152, 165-6, (DR1-30).
The following buses were converted into works vehicles:- AR 286, 288-290, 293, 283, 277, 280, 282.

With factories at both Bridlington and Blackburn, East Lancashire won a further order in 1954 to re-body 30 wartime Daimler CWA6 models. The batch had five-bay construction unlike the earlier but more modern-looking Albion-based version, and this example, DR6 (ex 110) shows off the black lining to good advantage. Note that display of the speed limit was still a legal requirement.

Crossley's standard immediate post-war design was adopted in almost completely unaltered form for C1. The DD42/3 chassis had been developed from a wartime prototype while the Crossley body based on Crossley-designed metal framing was also a fresh development, even though its frontal styling echoed Manchester Corporation's streamline design first seen in 1936. This official view shows the header tank used with the torque converter transmission, and the rear registration number location on the emergency door is also visible. The stepped waistline was justified by cross-bracing to support the platform, cantilevered from the body structure.

When this photograph was taken in February 1953, C1 was based at Larkfield Garage. A conventional clutch and gearbox had been fitted in 1950.

In 1958, C1 was sold to the Dodds-owned section of A.A. Motor Services Ltd of Ayr. Its mechanical specification was again altered by the fitting of a Gardner 5LW engine but the remainder of the vehicle continued largely as built until final withdrawal in 1963.

Chapter five:

The solitary Crossley

Bus enthusiasts were a rare breed in 1946. Those around then certainly did not broadcast this peculiar affinity for the commonplace mode of transport, and apart from comparing furtive notes with each other, there were few publications where news could be gleaned of forthcoming attractions. If a local newspaper published details of transport matters, so much the better, but in Glasgow's case, the announcement of the first post-war order for 68 buses did nothing to prepare our intrepid spotters for the sight and sound of the city's first post-war bus, after four years of utility style Daimler and Guy buses.

Among the first chassis manufacturers to return to normal production was Crossley Motors Ltd, by then based in Stockport although originating in Manchester. Following one prototype chassis in 1942-43, production started in earnest in 1946 with its DD42/3 design. It is not known if GCT intended to purchase several more — perhaps Crossley had invited the Department to try out the bus with the hope of more orders to follow. However, a Crossley DD42/3T with Crossley 56-seat body arrived in Glasgow in April 1947.

One can imagine the impact this vehicle had on enthusiasts and travellers alike. Not only did it have a new number (it had been assumed that the next bus into the fleet would be '829') — at first sight '01' — but it also displayed the particularly flamboyant curves that made a Crossley body instantly 'different' to even the most disinterested of passers-by. It heralded the new era of post-war transport in fine style.

The destination layout with a large number screen to the nearside, adjacent to a 'via' box, below an ultimate destination aperture had first been fitted to the experimental 'lightweight' trams 1001-1004 in 1940. On C1 this was incorporated at both front and rear, and indeed, became standard until 1956, although the rear display was no longer specified on the 1953 Albions and subsequent deliveries. Some older buses had this arrangement fitted at a convenient spell in the works — 92, 127, 131, 157, 646 and 724. The number, C1, also revealed the Department's plan to separate each type of bus by way of a prefix according to the chassis make. Incidentally, C1 along with Albions B1-24 had their rear registration numbers painted on the top deck rear emergency window like all pre-war and utility buses. This was removed to the more conventional area later, except on Albions 1-50 and the Leyland TD4s. Utility buses with unglazed emergency windows had the registration painted onto the lower-deck rear window.

C1 (EGA 75) was as revolutionary mechanically as it was visually, being fitted with a form of automatic transmission called a turbo transmitter, manufactured by Brockhouse. Several Crossley buses around this time were similarly equipped and were bought by Luton, Manchester and South Shields Corporations. This equipment meant a smoother start, eliminated clutch judder (or an apathetic driver) and made the driver's task much less arduous. Audibly, it sounded rather like today's modern buses fitted with Voith transmission, there being no characteristic 'through the box' progression when accelerating. 'Gearless' buses, it will be recalled, had

last been bought in 1935 with the arrival of the TD4c buses. After driver training had taken place, C1 was taken to Elderslie garage in the summer of 1947 and operated in splendid isolation. Before trolleybuses were introduced in April 1949, C1 was brought back to Glasgow and used to familiarise would-be trolley drivers with a vehicle that needed no gear changes, the nearest they could get to actual trolleybus operation.

As did most operators, GCT soon found that the turbo-transmitter was costly to maintain and operate so in 1950 the bus entered Larkfield Works to have this replaced by a conventional 4-speed gearbox and clutch. It was decided to keep the bus nearer home and so it resumed service from Larkfield. For many years it was the only bus allocated to service 31 (Carlton Place-Carmunnock) on Sundays — not the most frequent of routes even then! By 1957, scores of new deliveries were rendering large numbers of pre-war and 'odd' buses redundant, and C1 was withdrawn after ten years' service — a victim of 'non-standardisation'.

It saw further use, however, in Ayrshire, with the fleet of AA Motor Services, Ayr. The Department's connection with Crossley continued, however, as the first of 90 Crossley-bodied trolleybuses (TB35-124) were being delivered as C1 departed. There were also, of course, the AEC Regent Mark III's with Crossley bodies (A21-70) which were delivered in 1948, although no other Crossley bodies in the fleet had the characteristic outline of C1.

The 'laid-back' character of the Metro-Cammell body design with its straight sloping profile is most obvious in this view of A1 the first of the post-war delivery of AEC Regent III chassis with this make of bodywork, taken at Mosspark terminus. The body outline was largely as built by Metro-Cammell for various fleets since 1933, though this version had more modern glazing. The open cab windscreen was a sure sign of summer weather. The quaint Corporation Lighting Department lamp-post was a familiar sight in most pre-war housing schemes.

A61 was one of fifty AEC Regent III's with Crossley bodies, delivery of which began in 1948. It is pictured a few years later in the company of Leyland L27 at the former Govan Cross terminus in Greenhaugh Street. Though derived from the same body design as the complete Crossley bus, C1, the styling here becomes more orthodox, with unusually flat front panels.

One of Glasgow's most familiar suburbs must be Springburn, with its proud connection with transport of all types. The row of tenements at Springburn Station conceals the famous Hyde Park Works where locomotives were built for a world market. A79, one of 20 Regent IIIs with bodywork by Northern Coachbuilders dating from 1948, is dwarfed by its surroundings on a journey to Muirend, soon to be partly replaced by trolleybuses. The 37 remained one of the best-used services long after the wholesale closedown of the railway works.

By 1951, it had been decided to switch production of Glasgow orders for bus bodies placed with MCW back to Weymann. This time, however, it was the Metro-Cammell style of body design that was adopted, doubtless to maintain standardisation and acceptable when 100 bodies were required. Here, A224 represents this last batch of Regent Mark IIIs and is pictured in Govan Road. Exposed radiator buses could gain extra cooling air by simply opening the bonnet panels, but they seldom closed properly after a time! Flashing indicators have been added.

Chapter six: Post-war Regents

As GCT's policy was to favour products from AEC, it was to be expected that any post-war orders would reflect this. The AEC factory at Southall, Middlesex, had commenced post-war production with the Regent Mark II model which was mechanically very similar to the immediate pre-war buses Glasgow Corporation had purchased from 1937 to 1940. Concurrently, the factory was producing the famous 'RT' chassis for London Transport, which featured a much lower bonnet line, air-brakes, air-operated preselective gearbox and more powerful engine. It was hoped that provincial operators would follow London's lead by placing orders for this type, by then called the Regent Mark III, though the production version intended for operators outside London, originally designated O961/2, did not have the lower bonnet line.

A glance at the post-war orders for GCT reveals that the Department wasted no time in placing orders with AEC for 20 chassis in November 1945, and 70 in 1946. It is tempting to speculate on the possibility of the initial 20 being of the Mk II type or even RTs! It is noteworthy that the merits of the more elaborate specification of the Regent III appealed to Glasgow — perhaps significantly a picture of a pre-war GCT Regent, suitably retouched, had been used in AEC's first post-war leaflet for the model when no O961/2 version had yet been completed. However, the first post-war Regent buses to appear for GCT were from the batch ordered with Northern

Coachbuilders bodies (A71-90) — A71 in June followed by A21 — a Crossley-bodied example — in August 1948. In the same year, AEC changed the designation of these chassis to 9612E and the remaining AEC Regent Mk III's delivered to Glasgow Corporation were thus designated.

Crossley was better known for its 'own brand' buses, but the 50 bodies for Glasgow did not feature the usual Crossley styling and were of a more restrained appearance. Northern Coachbuilders supplied 20 bodies to their 1948 style, and these, together with Daimlers D1-20, built a year later, were the only examples ordered from the Newcastle firm. Early in the 1950s, the company ceased production and closed down. The choice of bodybuilders reflected the need for operators to 'shop around' after the war, as the demand for new vehicles outstripped the output of many of the 'traditional' suppliers, and delays were inevitable. The original order for 20 Regents with MCCW bodies was late in completion and A1-20 entered service in 1949, three years after the initial contract. Since the AEC chassis designation was changed in 1948, this batch had the later numbers, therefore were later chassis, so perhaps the bodybuilder was not entirely to blame for late delivery. AEC had given top priority to London Transport because they were alleged to be a special case.

Unfortunately, A8 could barely have been a year old when it was involved in one of the most horrific accidents in

GCT's history. Fully laden, it was proceeding along Great Western Road at Beaconsfield Road on 24th May 1950 bound for Rutherglen, when a spring fractured, causing the vehicle to topple on to its nearside straddling the roadway in the path of a Standard tram (89) travelling westwards. Number 89 ploughed into A8's top deck, killing seven passengers and injuring 43. Most of the top deck was destroyed, but after some months the bus was rebuilt.

Pre-war Glasgow orders for MCW (Metro-Cammell Weymann) bodywork had been handled by the Weymann factory. The immediate post-war orders were fulfilled by the other MCW partner, Metropolitan-Cammell Carriage and Wagon Co Ltd (MCCW), whose design for A1-20 and subsequent batches had the characteristic sloping front design which had its origins in the early 'thirties, and in some respects was considered dated by the late 'forties. While it was most common on AEC chassis, Glasgow placed similar bodies on Albions B25-48, which to the writer's mind did seem an unhappy combination. Later deliveries of Regent III buses had bodies labelled 'Weymann' but were almost identical to the MCCW product, the last 27 being fitted with heaters when new.

With the delivery of the last Mark IIIs in 1952, purchases of AEC buses ceased for the moment, but a year later, a lightweight Regent Mk III (7194 H) was inspected (*Chapter 13*) and operated on service 2 in City of Oxford livery. This demonstrator had a synchromesh gearbox and therefore was non-standard as far as GCT was concerned though the 7.7-litre engine was of the size used in pre-war GCT Regents. In 1954, a more radical change to Regent production took place when AEC introduced the Mark V version at Earls Court. Glasgow placed an order for 75 chassis in April. As the 'new look' front was gaining popularity, this feature was an optional extra for customers buying the Mark V, but not all of them took up the offer. Glasgow's new Regents (A266-340) were very special. GCT specified the Gardner 6LW engine, vacuum-assisted brakes and spring-operated preselective gearboxes: in fact, similar in name only to the previous Regents! Designated D2RV6G, only 80 of this chassis were built, the other five going to Aberdeen Corporation. Another special feature, the wider radiator grille, introduced on the Mark V buses, was replaced on the Glasgow (and Aberdeen) examples by a painted pressing with vertical strips. Liverpool Corporation had a similar grille on its Regent Vs, but the nearside mudguard was different. It is not clear why Gardner engines should have been ordered, as at the time there were only five remaining wartime Guy Arabs and D67 with this unit. Fifty Daimler buses with Gardner units were, admittedly, on order so one would expect that standardisation was uppermost in the minds of the engineers. On the other hand, 265 AEC engines had operated successfully and 25 Leyland PD2/25s were on order, but the Gardner's reputation for fuel economy was a strong factor at a time of rising costs.

The bodies were less unusual, being built by W. Alexander (49) and Weymann (26). They were the last to have traditional polished wood interior finish as well as the three-piece destination layout, although this feature had been omitted from the rear of the 1953 Weymann Albions and subsequent double-deckers. (Many older vehicles had them painted over and often removed completely when the opportunity arose). The Alexander/Weymann AECs A266-314

had a virtually identical appearance to the true Weymann products D68-116 and A315-340, but they were not nearly so solidly put together. They had to be called into Larkfield Works to have interior lining panels refixed to eliminate incessant rattling which soon arose after some running over sett-paved streets. The interior finish was also inferior and the Stirling firm used a slightly lighter stained oak for trimming, together with a lighter colour of chocolate (ie 'milk' instead of 'plain') for painting around the window panes. On the other hand, D67, the 1954 Motor Show Daimler (*Chapter 8*), was not as well turned out as D21-60 nor TG1-5 (1953 trolleybuses) which were thoroughbred Alexander bodies. The moral, no doubt, is that each firm should have stuck to building its own designs!

A further spate of demonstrators visited the city in 1957. Two AEC buses—88 CMV and 159 JHX—came north, being used on services 2 and 11 respectively. While the former had a synchromesh gearbox, 159 JHX, which was slightly older, featured the newly-introduced 'Mono-control' gear change, with two-pedal control and an electric gearchange lever on the steering column. After two years of demonstration work, 159 JHX found itself in the fleet of 'King Alfred', Winchester.

Semi-automatic transmission was gaining popularity with many larger provincial municipal fleets, whose ex-tram drivers were making the changeover to bus driving. The two-pedal control systems, Daimler 'Daimatic', Leyland 'Pneumo-cyclic' and AEC 'Mono-control' made the driver's task easier and GCT standardised on this equipment from 1956 onwards. Drivers thus trained by the driving schools at Larkfield and Knightswood obtained licences for semi-automatic psv's only.

After regulations permitting the use of 30ft.-long vehicles became effective in July 1956, larger capacity buses gained considerable popularity. In 1958 AEC produced a new chassis called the Bridgemaster and Glasgow Corporation

Transport used a demonstrator (76 MME) on service 11, but none was purchased. The tram replacement programme called for 229 forward-entrance buses each seating 72 passengers and the order was given to both AEC and Leyland to provide these vehicles. The unusual number of 89 Regent V buses with 'Mono-control' transmission amounted to AEC's share and delivery began in 1960. This joint order was equally noteworthy in that it represented the largest swing away from the rear platform bus by a city operator—headlines in the city's evening papers announced 'Monster Buses Arrive in Glasgow'.

From 1956 on, W. Alexander (Coachbuilders) Ltd had a monopoly on all GCT purchases until 1974 and the front-entrance bodies were similar to the Edinburgh example displayed at the 1957 Motor Show. While its Leyland counterpart L398 was displayed inside Earls Court in 1960, A351 was in the demonstration park, being fitted with plastic interior panels in comparison with the spartan painted metal interior finish which characterised the remainder. The bodies were identical to the Leyland PD3s apart from having electrically-powered doors—the Leylands had air-operated ones. Very early in their lives, these Alexander bodies gave rise to problems associated with the front entrance. Three steps were needed to gain access to the lower saloon and, when new, they were 'scalloped' to allow the four-leaf doors to fold inwards on each side. It is presumed that there had been instances where passengers' feet had been trapped as the doors opened and that the 'scalloped' steps had proved to be a safety hazard. Modifications were made to provide full width steps and, to permit free movement of the doors, rectangular apertures were cut into the leaves. These were provided with rubber flaps which, inevitably, broke off and were not replaced.

The rain guttering above the door was originally curved downwards on either side of the doorway. As a result, when buses pulled into stops in heavy rain,

Crossley-bodied A61, again, by now repainted into its last colour scheme when photographed heading citywards in Great Western Road. Following is a Leyland Titan from the Alexander empire and 'Coronation' tram 1185 about to turn right into Park Road. The 'Via' screen on the bus must surely have been a late survivor.

Latterly, the Regent V models with Gardner engines were based at Knightswood, but, when new, at least one example, A315, the first of the Weymann buses, was allocated to Larkfield. It is seen at Carmunnock, sporting short-lived wheel nut guard rings, soon after entering service in 1955.

A295, an Alexander-bodied Regent V in its final livery, turns from Bothwell Street into Hope Street. This right turn was eliminated under the city's 1963 one-way street scheme which involved extensive service re-routings. Both the Weymann and Alexander built versions of the Gardner-engined Regent had bodywork of Weymann design, basically a five-bay version of the curved-profile outline which had been favoured by most Weymann customers in the earlier post-war period but which was by then generally giving way to the lightweight Orion styles.

water flowed forward and into the path of waiting passengers. The guttering was altered and straightened out at the front bulkhead; both 'A' and 'L' class vehicles were modified. These bodies also had hopper windows on both decks; earlier W. Alexander rear-entrance buses had sliding windows in the lower saloon. Soon, after being exposed to damp, smoky conditions, the fasteners perished and the hopper windows opened and closed at will, according to the road conditions!

By the 'seventies, the spartan specification was beginning to tell and body movement was apparent around the forward staircase, front and rear domes worked loose and vertical grab poles had a tendency to work their way through the lower saloon floor. Like the lowbridge W. Alexander 30ft. long bodies, a full load upstairs caused the lower saloon ceiling to rise and fall as the bus lurched over the indifferent road surfaces. It was not unknown for the AEC buses to lose their front grilles while in service and, in some instances, they operated without them.

GCT had originally asked for Gardner 6LW engines for the 89 Mark V Regents, presumably to standardise the AEC fleet. It was claimed, however, that the extra length needed for such engines could not be accommodated in the space between the front grille and bulkhead. The 1956 Regent Mark V buses had the same front end dimensions into which the Gardner engine fitted, though only just! Whatever the excuse, the AEC AV590 was supplied and introduced another range of spares to the stores. Home garages for AEC buses were Knightswood and Ibrox and all the Gardner-engined Mk Vs were based at Knightswood. Elderslie had been allocated some new Regents IIIs. The front-entrance 'A's were split between Knightswood and Possilpark until their withdrawal, although some Mk IIIs

found themselves at Parkhead—always an Albion stronghold—in their last years. In 1962 some Regents from the 1960 batch were transferred to Langside to operate the short-lived service 70 (Kings Park Station-Castlemilk). This was the second attempt by GCT to provide an 'interlink' service, but Glasgow passengers disliked changing from train to bus and the service was withdrawn exactly six months later on 5th May 1963. The buses were returned from the then predominantly Daimler garage—Langside—to their home base.

November 1967 saw the withdrawal of the last of the Mark III Regents from passenger service; some of the first to be delivered survived the longest. Body swaps were carried out three years previously when the chassis of A86 and A219 received the bodies from A17 and A263 respectively. A32 was used by Glasgow Airport for a year before its withdrawal. Alternative employment was also found for A29 as a mobile clinic, finally moving to the driving school. Several were retained as snowploughs for two years until the Cleansing Department took over the

duties of gritting and snow clearing. The 1955-56 Regents did not last so long, and after some were used as learners, all were sold by 1970.

The remaining Mark Vs were now lost in a multitude of Leyland-engined buses—very much the poor relations and by 1973 in a very sorry state. No more overhauls were carried out on them and only a few received the new Greater Glasgow PTE livery. They were sold by 1975—two years before their Leyland cohorts. One vehicle, A350, was retained for conversion into a mobile training bus with display areas downstairs and a cinema area on top. Initially, it was used for metrication training in 1975-76, then as a publicity bus for the forthcoming modernisation of the Underground. After several years of dis-use, it was sold in 1983 for private preservation.

The AEC era in Glasgow had ended and the familiar blue triangle was no more. AEC came into the Leyland empire in 1962 and although continuing as a separate concern, gradually lost more and more of its independence before the Southall works closed in 1979.

A1-265 had 56-seat bodies, A266-340 had 60 seats, A341-429 had 72 seats.
A1-265 had 9612E chassis except A21-38, 40, 42, 56 which were O961/2.
A1-20, 91-165 had MCCW and A166-265, 315-40 had Weymann bodies; Crossley built for A21-70 and Alexander for A266-314, 341-429.
A341-429 had 2D2RA chassis.
Registrations: A1-20 were registered EGA 55-74. A21-340 were FYS 121-265, 349-448, 572-620, 621-646. A341-429 were SGD 491-579.
The 'reversed' livery was applied to A46, 58, 106, 108, 190, 219, 347, 415-6, 426.
A39 lower saloon front seats faced inwards, A137 had non-standard layout of opening windows upper saloon. A393-4 had non-opening driver's windscreens.
The following were used as snowploughs (s) or Learner buses (L) for some time before withdrawal:-
(L) A3, 4, 8, 19, 20, 44, 49, 51-3, 67, 78, 86, 118, 124, 131, 133, 144, 146-7, 159-60, 162, 178, 181-2, 187, 207, 217, 258, 261, 265-6, 271, 277, 280, 285-6, 288, 292-311, 314-6, 318, 320-1, 326, 332.
(s) A24, 38, 66, 71, 109, 151, 155, 158, 192, 201, 203, 216, 222, 240-242, 198-200, 232.

(Above) When delivered in 1947, the 24 Albion Venturer CX19 models with Roberts bodywork that represented the first major post-war addition to the fleet had recessed windows as used by Midland Red. However, following an accident with newly-delivered B17 for which the driver blamed poor visibility due to the heavy frames of the windscreen, the bodies were altered as shown on B21. At the junction of Duke Street and Cumbernauld Road, Roberts-bodied Venturer B84 follows under the complicated tram and trolleybus overhead layout.

(Centre) Views of buses in garage yards often provided comparisons which were hard to obtain while they were in service. This view at Parkhead illustrates the curvaceous Brockhouse design (of Park Royal origin) on B108, built in 1950, alongside the severe Roberts product, represented by B8. The latter shows evidence of a re-built destination screen box. The later CX37S chassis with its 9.9-litre engine, differed only slightly from the 9.0-litre CX19 version.

(Below) Albion Venturers, with their conventional clutch and gearbox, were used to provide training to full PSV standards before the Department changed to semi-automatic licences only. After passenger use, Albions were also often retained for some time as snowploughs. B29 passes 'Coronation' tram 1213 in Sauchiehall Street and shows off the rather clumsy combination of MCCW body and Scotstoun-built chassis that did not really appear 'comfortable'.

Chapter seven: Albion twilight

The city's fleet of pre-war Albion Venturers had amounted to some 130 buses plus seven single-deckers. With Albion Motors practically on GCT's doorstep at Scotstoun, it could be safely assumed that further Albions would be taken into stock after the war. By 1946 only a few of the 1935-36 batches remained in the fleet, and, once production started again with a post-war version of the CX19 chassis, Glasgow Corporation placed an order for 48. The post-war chassis differed slightly from previous models principally in some changes in the type of gears used in the gearbox. There were to be no sophisticated pre-selective gears nor automatic transmission from Albion and, until the end of Venturer production—indeed until the introduction of the Lowlander—Albion remained staunchly committed to the manual gearchange and clutch pedal.

No Scottish-built bodies were purchased for the first Albions (B1-48), as Charles Roberts of Wakefield and MCCW, Birmingham, were selected to build 56-seat double-deckers. Delivery was painfully slow, which was to dog all immediate post-war orders, but especially Albion's bodybuilders. By the end of 1947 only fifteen of the Yorkshire-made products had appeared. However, 1948 saw the balance arrive. The first, and probably all, of the B25-48 batch entered service on New Year's Day 1949. These Birmingham-built buses had a pronounced sloping front, whose ancestry could be traced back to the early 'thirties. This design of MCCW body was much more commonly placed on AEC chassis. The Albions for Glasgow had much higher lower-deck skirt panels than the AECs and showed off much of the underside equipment such as the fuel tank! As a result, they seemed to be rather ungainly.

CX19 production stopped in 1948 when Albion introduced the CX37S model offering a larger engine (9.9-litre). The model was introduced at the Commercial Motor Show 1948 as B49, the first of 40 CX37S models with Roberts bodies for GCT. As might be expected, B49 had several 'Show' features such as fluorescent lighting (removed in 1950), stainless steel handrails and fittings, Dunlop rubber wings and mudguards and a very pronounced curved front which was not a feature of the rest of the batch. Metal louvres above the side windows were also fitted (B52-4 also had these). The curved front on B49 was eliminated by the bodybuilders before delivery to Glasgow. Delivery was very slow and it was three years before the order was completed. Charles Roberts was engaged in building 35 tramcar bodies for Sheffield Corporation, as no other builder would attempt such an order, and this, no doubt, held up production. Glasgow's Albions and the Sheffield trams had very similar interior fittings.

A further batch of 25 CX37S chassis was ordered and it was intended to have the bodies built at the Bus Works, the Corporation having been granted powers to do so in 1946. However, as will be seen (*Chapter 8*) the Works was fully committed in building the single-deck Daimlers and, with no sign of any acceleration in the output of new bodies, it was obvious that no further work could be considered. MCCW was given an order for 25 frames in September 1947, but this order was either cancelled or postponed until later. The Department had to look for other builders and Croft, Scottish Aviation and Brockhouse were given the contracts for ten, five and ten respectively. The first two named builders, it will be recalled from *Chapter 4*, were the suppliers of bodies for reconditioned chassis. The third manufacturer, from West Bromwich, had recently opened a factory at Clydebank in 1948. It had a trade agreement with Park Royal and bodies built by Brockhouse were to Park Royal design.

In 1950, Brockhouse provided buses for other municipal fleets in Scotland—three deckers on AEC chassis for Dundee, plus ten Daimlers the next year. Fifteen single-deck bodies on Bristol chassis and seventeen Regent double-deckers were completed for Edinburgh. Aberdeen received ten Daimler double-deckers and ten Crossley saloons. Glasgow's Albions B89-98 (Croft), B109-113 (Scottish Aviation) and B99-108 were delivered by 1950.

Although by no means a frequent occurrence, the city saw another overturning accident on 21st August 1950, again with a brand new bus, this time B100. Whilst travelling along Shettleston Road on service 1A, the bus collided with a telegraph pole and overturned, injuring 30 passengers. The tramway overhead was pulled down and delays were experienced for some time. It appears Glasgow's new buses had to hit the headlines in a spectacular way, as this incident took place only three months after A8's.

Regulations governing the

In 1950, it became legal to operate buses of 8 feet in width in the United Kingdom without the need for special permission on a route-by-route basis that had applied since 1946. Albion Motors responded to this edict by offering what had been an export chassis for the home market. Twenty-five CX37SW buses were supplied and, if the Department had not been overruled, its own workshops would have provided the bodies. As it was, Weymann won the contract although this meant a three-year delay in entering service. B131 passes the Tolbooth Steeple at Glasgow Cross on a route long associated with Albion vehicles.

dimensions of British psvs had altered in 1950 to permit full-scale operation of buses to a width of 8 feet. In 1951 Albion had produced an 8ft. wide chassis, the CX37SW, mainly for export (where such restrictions did not apply) and GCT bought 25. Again, it was the Corporation's intention to make full use of the available expertise and manpower within the Transport Department. However, due to continuing delays, it was decided in June of that year that MCW would build the bodies (modifying the order for frames not previously constructed?). This was bitterly opposed by the NUVB who complained about jobs being taken from local craftsmen. The Corporation deferred the decision until September, but the previous resolution was upheld, and MCW (Weymann) was given the order. The chassis had been stored in Knightswood garage, but in 1953 were despatched to Weymann for bodying. Glasgow's last Albion double-deckers were the first batch of 8ft. wide buses and were used to test operation of such vehicles in new housing areas. B138 had the distinction of being the last Albion-engined double-decker to be built.

One final Albion bus was delivered to GCT in 1952. This was based on an experimental chassis (designated KP71NW), one of two built with eight cylinder horizontally-opposed 9.7-litre underfloor engines. The body was built by Scottish Aviation with seating for 39, and a rear entrance/front exit arrangement (the opposite, it will be noted, from DS1-43). Theoretically, there was room for up to seventeen standing passengers. GCT agreed to operate this bus on a trial basis and it was sent to Knightswood garage for use at Clydebank. BS1 (FYS 495) was the first Glasgow bus to have a five-speed

gearbox but 5th gear was blanked off and not used. In 1959, the bus was sold to Albion Motors. By this time, the policy of having separate entrances and exits was losing favour from the (then) current thinking.

As the years progressed, the Albion vehicles were herded together at Parkhead. As they were the only remaining buses with manual gearboxes by 1960, their withdrawal could not have been difficult to foresee. The Department wished to train bus drivers on semi-automatics only. Having passed their test, it was assumed they were less likely to desert GCT for other companies where a 'full' licence was necessary. Many Albions found further employment in independent fleets in Scotland and some were retained as snowploughs. When the Transport Museum was being planned, using part of the former Coplawhill tram works building, the desire to exhibit a locally-built motorbus was expressed. At that time, a few remained in service and B92 was set aside for that purpose. The chassis and body were built in the

Glasgow area, including the tyres—by India at Inchinnan! B92 was duly installed for the opening in 1964. On occasions, it was allowed out and used in processions although not as a psv.

Glasgow's own bus builder, Albion, was no longer represented in the fleet. Despite the revival of the Albion name for the Lowlander (Chapter 13) no more Albion double-deckers were built for GCT. Having been taken over by Leyland in 1951, it was surprising that the company retained its individualistic approach to psv chassis for so long afterwards, though the heavy-duty passenger models were dropped almost immediately. Certainly, GCT had no traffic work suitable for Albion single-deckers such as the Viking or Nimbus, and the introduction of the Leyland Atlantean proved the death knell for most front-engined chassis manufacturers. We might have seen something different had Leyland allowed their Atlantean chassis to be marketed as 'Albion' in Scotland, rather than simply have a special badge introduced.

Registrations: EGA 7-54 were allocated to B1-48, FYS 266-305 (B49-88), EGA 76-100 (B89-113) and FYS 496-520 (B114-138).
The chassis types were: CX19 (B1-48), CX37S (B49-113) and CX37SW (B114-138).
The bodies were built by Croft for B89-98, Brockhouse for B99-108 and Scottish Aviation for B109-113. The latter had inward-facing front lower saloon seats. Other bodybuilders were Roberts (B1-24, 49-88), MCCW (B25-48) and Weymann (B114-138).
B71, 84, 91, 114-7, 119-126, 128-131, 133-8 were used as snowploughs after passenger service.
B29, 34, 104 were used as Learner buses after passenger service.

(Left) Nicknamed 'Bessie', BS1 saw only seven years' service. This unusual view, taken when new, shows the rear screen display, a feature missing from the GCT-bodied Daimlers and Leyland Worldmasters.

(Below) The very narrow doorways on the Scottish Aviation body rather restricted passenger movement. BS1 was often used on the local Clydebank services until their abandonment in 1955. The legal lettering has been wisely positioned to avoid spills from the fuel filler point.

The general standard of finish inside post-war buses around the late 'forties was high and continued until the 'fad' for lightweight designs in the mid 'fifties. This view of B107, one of the Brockhouse bodied CX37S buses reveals Alhambrinal ceiling, polished wooden framework, advert frames, fare stage holder and moquette seats — giving an air of opulence equal to the 'Coronation' trams. The GCT route plate holder can be seen fixed to the nearside window. This held the metal 'running' or route number.

'Sure as the Sunrise'

Albion number 820 of 1940 lost its original Wishaw-built Pickering body in 1952. Along with 29 other Venturer CX19s, it was rebodied by East Lancashire Coachbuilders, becoming BR27. It operated in this new form until 1960. Road safety doesn't seem to concern the passenger hanging off the open rear platform, a feature of Glasgow's double-deck service buses until withdrawal of the last Leylands PD2s in 1977. Like the cover view, the photograph was taken at Anniesland Cross.

Partial body repaints were a well-remembered feature of the transitional period between the old Corporation Transport green, cream and orange colours and the duller spray-painted livery. Parkhead Garage was the most consistent 'offender', being represented here by its B52, a 1949 Albion Venturer CX37S with bodywork by Charles Roberts of Wakefield. A completely repainted B78 follows closely behind B52 in George Square on 25th April 1962.

Croft-bodied Venturer B92 is the sole survivor of Glasgow Corporation's 'native' Albion bus fleet. Following withdrawal from service in 1963, it was set aside for display in the city's first Museum of Transport which opened in April 1964. B92 made occasional outside trips, one of which took place on 10th May 1975 when it participated in a procession to mark the 800th anniversary of the granting of Glasgow's Burgh Charter. B92 is now a permanent exhibit in the Kelvin Hall Museum of Transport.

The largest single post-war order till then for one type of vehicle was placed in May 1948 (*Appendix D*). This materialised in 1951/52 as A166-265, one hundred AEC Regent Marks IIIs with Weymann bodywork built to the basic MCCW design seen on B25-48, A1-20 and A91-165. A262, pictured on a well-cambered Shieldhall Road, was withdrawn in 1966.

Although single-deckers have formed a small proportion of the Glasgow bus fleet, their distinctiveness has usually made up for any lack of numbers. No exception to this rule is one of 30 Leyland Royal Tiger Worldmaster 'export' chassis fitted with Coplawhill-made dual doorway bodywork on Weymann frames between 1956 and 1958. Seen at Eastwood Toll shortly after delivery, LS6 was rebuilt in 1961 to retain only the front doorway. Following withdrawal, LS6 (together with LS1, 7, 8 and 15) ran for Southend Corporation between 1966 and 1972.

L126 was one of six new Corporation-bodied Leyland PD2/24s which emerged from Coplawhill Works in 1959 with an experimental light green and yellow livery separated by a black line. This break with tradition was dictated by the economics of spray painting and the version eventually decided on dispensed with the black line, separating the two colours with a 7in. cream band instead. St. Enoch Square itself has seen many radical changes over the past three decades with the disappearance of the railway station and hotel, and the Glasgow Air terminal with its SMT Bristol/ECW coaches, not forgetting the Western SMT bus stance.

The photographer proves the unwanted centre of attraction as he attempts to capture Glasgow's very first Alexander-bodied Leyland Atlantean on film. LA1, then based at Ibrox Garage, waits at the Priesthill terminus in April 1958. Special features visible in this rear view include the one-piece engine shroud and non-standard trafficators, These were subsequently modified to the 'Mark II' condition visible on LA1 today in the Kelvin Hall Museum of Transport.

Albion's final concerted effort to interest the Corporation Transport Department in buying a new 'local' product was the 'Lowlander', a low-floor version of the Leyland PD3. After Alexander-bodied 747 EUS was shown in GCT specification and livery at the 1961 Scottish Motor Show, it was placed on extended loan for twelve months, before repeating the process in the capital wearing Edinburgh colours. No orders came from either municipality and 747 EUS was sold to a Lancashire independent operator which was eventually absorbed by Ribble. It is pictured on trade plates outside the Scotstoun works of Albion Motors.

Dissatisfaction with the rather dismal spray-painted livery of 1959 (opposite page and above photo) led to an interesting experiment in the autumn of 1964 when 21 motorbuses and one trolleybus were painted in this 'reversed' colour scheme. While it suited flat-sided vehicles like Alexander-bodied AEC Regent V A416 (seen at a less than immaculate Drumchapel terminus), it was not so successful on older vehicles with raised body mouldings. Reaction was apparently adverse and the scheme was quickly abandoned.

The PTE Years

In 1975, the 800th anniversary of Glasgow's Burgh Charter provided the perfect opportunity for the Greater Glasgow PTE to reintroduce the bus tours which had been a popular feature of the city's bus fleet in pre-war years. Pictured on *Glasgow 800* tour duties in Kelvin Way, PDR1/1 Atlantean LA418 displays the special 'Leyland-Albion Atlantean' badge fitted when new. Full details of other City Tour buses are given in *Appendix II*.

Poor reliability of the PDR1/1 Atlanteans in particular had created interest in alternative chassis configurations. In 1974/75, two completely different marques made their debut in Glasgow. Scania-MCW Metropolitans M1-40 were the first non-Leyland/Alexander products bought for more than a decade. In July 1976, M11 and M40 take an over-generous layover on the newly-introduced Centre Circle service in Parliamentary Road. They are in the Greater Glasgow PTE's first livery style. All 40 had gone by 1982.

Contrasting liveries from the final years of PTE bus operations. Ailsa-Volvo AV11 (right) is in the penultimate style, with *Trans-Clyde* logo, introduced in 1980, while the first Ailsa AV1 (left) displays the 'Strathclyde Red' and black livery with regional council logo applied as standard to the entire fleet from 1983 until the cessation of direct bus operations three years later. These Scottish-assembled buses — with their distinctive panoramic windows — have withstood the test of heavy city work. AV1's distinctive peaked front and rear domes (a feature shared with AV2 and 3) are clearly visible.

Daimler had initially developed its post-war CVD6 model in single-deck form, although that maker's business had long had the major emphasis on double-deckers and the type was offered in versions to suit either form of bodywork. Glasgow turned away from the AEC and Albion single-deck models favoured in 1939-40, both still available in similar form in 1946-7, and chose the CVD6 for its new single-deck fleet. The first to be completed, DS43, built on a Daimler stock chassis, is posed with Department staff to show off the front-entrance and rear-exit layout of its GCT-built body. Sadly, none of these well-appointed buses has been preserved.

Chapter eight:

The 'Coventry Collection'

Until 1949, Daimler buses (or to be more accurate — Transport Vehicles (Daimler) Ltd) had not featured greatly in GCT's fleet. Only 25 COG6 buses had been purchased pre-war from choice as opposed to the 169 wartime utility chassis which had been *allocated* to the Department. In December 1946, GCT ordered 20 CVD6 chassis. This type was introduced by Daimler once peacetime production got underway, and was more a refined version of the rugged wartime CWA6 and CWD6 buses, incorporating the preselective gearchange together with the latter's Daimler-manufactured 8.6-litre diesel engine. Only five of the wartime buses built by Daimler and allocated to Glasgow had Daimler engines — the rest had AEC or Gardner units.

In 1948 Copenhagen was host to a British exhibition and Daimler requested that Glasgow provide an example from its fleet. Having had no post-war deliveries, the next best thing was a utility Daimler, one with a Daimler engine, of course, and No. 157 was earmarked for the trip. The Brush body was modified to include the post-war destination screen layout, semaphore trafficators, a coat of arms on the upper-deck panels and 'City of Glasgow' fleetname above the lower saloon windows. Along with examples from Nottingham, Birmingham, Bradford and other towns, Glasgow's Daimler left on 1st September 1948 for Copenhagen

and clocked up some 4,124 miles before returning on 13th October. Incidentally, these double-deckers from Great Britain were the first of this type to be seen in Copenhagen.

While No. 157 was being prepared for its European trip, proposals were being discussed nearer home on the replacement vehicles for the single-deck tramcars on Kilbowie Road, Clydebank, where a low railway bridge prevented double-deck operation. In 1947, the decision had been taken to replace the cut-down Standard cars 'as soon as replacement vehicles became available', and the Department set about designing a fleet of single-deck buses. The General Manager, Mr E. R. L. Fitzpayne was determined to try continental practices on the travelling public. The opportunity to utilise single-deckers of this type then came to light with the passengers on tram service 20 already being used to one-deck vehicles! In March 1947, an order was placed for 43 Daimler CVD6 chassis; the single-deck bodies were to be built by the Department at Larkfield bus works, using Metal Sections frames.

Designed by the Corporation Transport Department, the bodies had separate rear exits and front entrances, with seats for 33 passengers. Folding power-operated doors were fitted and, with a 6ft. 7in. headroom, well-appointed interior and 'Glasgow Corporation Transport' above the

windows, they were a splendid addition to the fleet. However, production was slow. DS43, in a somewhat Irish fashion, was first to appear in 1948, followed by batches of ten in each subsequent year until 1952, with DS42 arriving in 1953! A revised livery was applied to DS43 (*Chapter 15*). The last two buses had 28 seats fitted from their inception until 1961, when they were altered to conform with the others.

The 20 CVD6 buses ordered in December 1946 materialised in 1949 as D1-20 with Northern Coachbuilders 56-seat wooden-framed bodies. A further batch of CVD6s were ordered in 1948 (D21-59) and entered service in 1950-51 with W. Alexander bodies. Around this time, Birmingham City Transport, who had purchased many Daimler buses, introduced the 'new look' front to its Daimler, Guy and Crossley double-deckers, concealing the familiar manufacturer's radiator. However, Glasgow was more traditionally minded in this respect and opted for the classic Daimler 'look'. Five more CVD6 chassis were bodied by Scottish Aviation (D61-65) and were similar to Albions B109-113, delivered the previous year.

Motor Shows have always provided an opportunity to introduce new features or advanced technical achievements, as is apparent throughout the story of the Glasgow bus. 1948 was no exception, and at London's Earls Court, a Daimler chassis was displayed which incorporated hydraulically-operated power steering, gearbox and brakes. Daimler at first designated this variation CVD650 and a 10.6-litre Daimler engine supplied the power. The large engine required a much wider radiator than previous models and was a good identification feature. Glasgow ordered one bus of this type and it was delivered in June 1951, complete with Alexander bodywork.

This was the first example of the new model, by then officially the CD650, to be supplied to a municipal fleet and Glasgow can thus claim to have been the first such operator in Britain to have a bus with power steering in service, though two for Tailby & George Ltd, the Derbyshire independent, had been supplied in March-April.

Also at Earls Court in 1950 were three luxury coaches bodied by the Norwich firm of Mann Egerton. London Transport had purchased many single-deck Leyland Tigers and AEC Regals in 1946 with Mann Egerton bodies and, although diversifying into the luxury coach market, Mann Egerton produced one double-deck bus for GCT, mounted it on a Daimler CVD6 chassis, and displayed it in London. Special exhibition features included a platform handrail which warned the driver by means of an illuminated sign in his cab of passengers remaining on the rear platform. The body, incorporating more than a hint of London Transport practice, was 8ft. wide (on a 7ft. 6in. wide chassis) and was Glasgow's first example of that width. Only a handful of double-deck bodies were built by Mann Egerton and none were for GCT. When the Show bus was delivered to Glasgow, the fleet number transfers 'D66' were added front and rear and the bus entered service.

'One-off' examples in a highly standardised fleet seldom last the 'full term' and tend to be disposed of when the first opportunity arises. By 1960, the Mann Egerton body was in need of replacement. The other 'odd' Daimler, D60, was also non-standard—or at least the chassis was—so it was arranged to marry D60's body to the chassis of D66 and scrap the remaining 'bits'.

In an era when front-engined single-deckers were about to be made obsolete almost overnight with the move to underfloor engines, many manufacturers turned to such examples which allowed entrances to be placed directly alongside the driver, gave the maximum seating capacity permitted and, more important to the future, could be used without conductors. Just as Albion was experimenting with two underfloored examples, Daimler was producing its version, to be called the 'Freeline', built for both home and export markets. More prolific than the Albion example, the Freeline was, however, rarely found in municipal fleets and GCT agreed to have one on trial in 1952. Scottish Aviation was asked to produce a body similar to that built for BS1 but when it was announced that this would not be possible, W. Alexander received the order. A centre entrance/exit body was built to the Coronation coach style being produced for other operators, with 32 seats and room for standees. The extra wide centre opening was without doors. Dual entrance/exit bodies were a rarity from W. Alexander at this time, although in 1954 an example for Dundee Corporation (22) was built for one-man-operation; hence the close resemblance to the more popular and conventional design. Legally, it was on hire until 1954 when GCT purchased the bus from Daimler. In 1960, doors were fitted along with an additional four seats. DS44 remained in service for a

further two years before it, too, became a victim of the 'one-off' syndrome.

Earlier in this chapter, mention was made of the 'new look' fronts on Birmingham buses. In 1954, BCT No. 3132 was hired for GCT services 2 and 11. This was a Daimler CVG6 with Crossley 55-seat body to Birmingham specification complete with straight staircase, and its use anticipated Glasgow's purchase of a large fleet of similar vehicles. Keeping No. 3132 company was 3060, a Guy Arab Mk IV bus with an identical body to 3132, but by MCCW. Although none of this type of chassis was purchased, the bodywork bore a family resemblance to the bodies chosen by GCT for its CVG6 models—especially around the front top deck windows.

The first CVG6 bus (with Gardner engine) for Glasgow was D67 and it appeared at the 1954 Show in London with an 'odd' Alexander body with MCW framing. Gone was the traditional radiator. This and subsequent Daimlers had the tin fronts as standard. Some operators, having experienced this frontal feature, returned to the more traditional exposed radiators because mechanics found the new fronts most restrictive when working on the engine. The remaining 49 CVG6s of this batch (D68-116) had Weymann bodies like the 1955 Leylands and AEC deliveries. D95 entered service with unpainted body panels, very much in vogue at this time. Money could be saved by not painting buses, it was then thought, and, at least Edinburgh, Liverpool, Halifax Corporations and London Transport followed suit. D95 was also the first bus to receive flashing indicators (known as 'blinkers' then). Having been approved by the Ministry of Transport, these were quickly fitted to the rest of the batch and also the AECs which had brown plastic

The Tyneside firm of Northern Coachbuilders came into prominence in wartime and afterwards secured orders from quite a number of well-known operators until its demise in the early 'fifties. By 1958 these wooden-framed bodies, which still suffered from the continuing shortage of good timber, were showing a deterioration not found in all-metal ones. D13, one of 20 CVD6s so bodied in 1949 was on a busy run at Mosspark Boulevard among football traffic which included Western SMT Guys.

The crews on both D26, an Alexander-bodied CVD6, and the 1953 Daimler Freeline, also bodied by Alexander and numbered DS44, have time to stare at the photographer at the St. Enoch Square stance. The lack of covered accommodation for passengers is evident but with frequent services, such street furniture might have been considered unnecessary. This view also has captured a much-rebuilt 1936 Albion Valkyrie PW67 from the Dodds of Troon fleet, by then running with a second-hand Bellhouse Hartwell body and Leyland engine which was withdrawn in 1955.

strips fitted initially in place of the 'blinkers'. Earlier buses were also dealt with, including B114-138, but not the rest of the Albions nor the Daimler single-deckers DS1-43.

In October 1955, GCT ordered 150 buses to be delivered as required at a cost of £267,000. Eight months later, the bodywork contract was placed with W. Alexander (£360,000) but it was deferred for two weeks while the Corporation debated the use of Coplawhill car works, as the tramcar fleet declined. In September, therefore, it was decided that the car works would build 50 bus bodies per year in order to keep the remaining works' staff employed. Mr Fitzpayne stated that, as bus orders were taking two years to complete, further tram replacement vehicles should be ordered. The first of the W. Alexander order arrived in the form of D117-131 at the end of 1956, with 61-seat rear-entrance bodies. A triple track service number layout at the front over a one-line destination display became standard from then on, with a three-track number screen above the platform. Use was made, in later deliveries (D211-216 and D218 onwards), of glass fibre front and rear domes and corner panels. The GCT-built bodies were placed on Leyland chassis only (*Chapter 9*). By 1957, up to D216 had been built.

The first Motor Show in Scotland after the relaxation of regulations allowing 30ft. long two-axle double-deckers was in 1957, and Daimler chose its CVD6-30 example fitted with W. Alexander 73-seat body to be displayed in the Kelvin Hall. The features found on D60 in

1950 — power steering and the 10.6-litre engine — were repeated, although a fully-automatic gearbox replaced the preselective version. D217 had a modified fibreglass bonnet front, similar to a new design for Manchester Corporation, and this latter style, slightly narrower, became the standard for the remaining Daimler rear-entrance buses for Glasgow. While Edinburgh Corporation's show bus, a 30ft. long PD3/2 numbered 998, had a front entrance, Glasgow's D217, despite its extra length, retained a rear platform layout. Importance was given in the technical press to the heaters to be found on both decks of D217 — something almost taken for granted nowadays but only fitted to very few GCT buses in pre-Atlantean days.

A further 30ft. long Daimler was operated by GCT for a few months in 1959, this being VKV 99, with Willowbrook 74-seat body, and it was used on the 4/4A service until April. Translucent panels were fitted on the roof of the bus which, after demonstration duties, found its way to the fleet of McGill of Barrhead. A CVG6-30, it had become the first bus to have a Gardner 6LX engine when so fitted in 1958.

The final batch of 50 CVG6s had 27ft. long bodies of the standard 61-seat Alexander design, but with sliding doors to the driver's cab, rather than hinged ones. D218-242 were sent to Newlands garage to replace tram service 8 on 15th March 1959 (service 38). Although small in number, these last Daimler CVG6s for Glasgow were nevertheless interesting. This batch was

the last to be delivered in the traditional green, cream and orange with particularly durable paint finish. The remaining buses, D243-267, were painted yellow and green at W. Alexanders. They entered service in November 1959 on the tram service 14 replacement route (57). D263-267 were fitted with Daimler CD6 Mk VIII engines with BSA 100/200 turbo chargers. The return to Daimler engines was surprising. Although Daimler had introduced this engine with the turbocharger the previous year, only D263, 264 and 266 went on the road with the turbocharger fitted. By 1972, the Daimler engines had been changed to Gardner units 'in the interests of standardisation'.

The smooth running, quiet characteristics of the Daimler range of post-war buses remained part of the Glasgow scene until the 'sixties. By 1965, all the pre-1954 batches had gone, including the Daimler single-deckers. D68-116's demise was remarkable in that all 49 were de-licensed together in May 1968 and sold in 1969 in one fell swoop! Many Falkirk-bodied Daimlers were resurrected by a new Chief Engineer (Mr A. Westwell) after investigation into availability of all types in the early 'seventies. D217, which had lost its power steering in 1965 and Daimler engine three years later, had received a Gardner 6LW engine (believed to have been fitted to A273). It was sold in May 1978 after several years in storage, being subsequently purchased for private preservation.

A more mundane fate was in store for other Daimlers, although D197 was used as a garage shunter until 1978, three years after the rest had gone. The last recorded journey was made by D199 on service 12 in May 1975. Thought was given to the possibility of converting Daimler buses to Cummins engines — but this came to naught. Perhaps if they had forward entrances, this idea would have had more appeal. Some of the CVG6s from 1959 saw some further service in Aberdeen — a very rare event for ex-GCT vehicles. There they merged in comfortably with similar vehicles. However, the Daimler story is not quite complete.

When Leyland produced the Atlantean bus, Daimler was not slow in following by offering a similar design of chassis incorporating the Gardner engine as standard. The chassis was known as the Fleetline and soon built up a large clientele, notably in Birmingham, with the Scottish Bus Group and, later, in London. The Daimler company had in the past been keen for operators to try out its products, and often made 'one offs' to good effect — take GCT's D60, D217 and DS44, for example. In November 1962, it was thought vital to gain prestige orders for the new Fleetline bus in areas were the Atlantean had made a good start. GCT was invited to operate a Daimler Fleetline on a trial basis, to compare its operation with the Atlanteans. At the time, W. Alexander was building a batch of Fleetlines for the Midland Red company and intended to use a similarly finished body to Midland Red specification. W. Alexander, however, finished the bus in the standard Glasgow LA style, apart from the flat floor, which was a feature of 'highbridge' Fleetlines.

D268 entered service in May 1963 from Maryhill Garage. Later that year, on show at the Kelvin Hall, Daimler, obviously confident of further orders from GCT, exhibited a Fleetline in Glasgow livery with a similar 78-seat body by W. Alexander, which became 565 CRW. In October the Transport Committee agreed to purchase this bus, but the full Corporation asked them to reconsider the matter with the result that the bus remained a Daimler demonstrator until purchased by

Graham's of Paisley. D268 remained GCT's only Fleetline amongst hundreds of Atlanteans. After periods of disuse, it was eventually de-licensed at the end of 1974 and sold ... to Graham's in 1975!

The Daimler company came into the British Leyland Motor Corporation on its formation in 1968. Production of the Daimler Fleetline continued at Coventry until 1973 but from 1974 it officially became the Leyland Fleetline until production by them at Leyland ceased in 1981.

D60-66 had 56-seat bodies; D67-116 seated 60 passengers and D268 had 78 seats.
Fleetline D268 had a CRG6LX chassis.
Registrations were as follows:- D1-20 (FYS 101-120), D21-66 were FYS 449-494, D67-116 were FYS 522-571, D117-166 were FYS 927-976, D167-216, 218-267 were SGD 151-250, D217 is FYS 999, D268 was SGD 730. DS1-43 were FYS 306-348 and DS44 was FYS 521. D61-65, 67 lower saloon front seats faced inwards. D258 had glass fibre seats on top deck fitted 1967.
D19 was painted in reversed livery.
D10, 14, 23, 46, 176, DS2-3, 5, 8, 23, 36 were retained as Learner buses for some time after withdrawal.

D67 was another singular oddity in terms of bodywork though the chassis was a CVG6 with 'new look' front, this having become the standard specification by 1954, when it was built — operators were becoming more sensitive to running costs and the Gardner 6LW was hard to beat. The Alexander body, despite appearances, is described as having 'MCW-pattern framing' and the proportions between bulkheads suggest that this was of Weymann origin though the front and rear were clearly designed in Alexander's drawing office. Curiously, a recessed sloping windscreen was fitted originally and later removed, just as with the 1947 Roberts-bodied Albions — the front mudguards also changed from orange to black, as seen in the High Street view. The interior was transitional, with a mixture of wood trim and the later all-metal finishes that were to follow.

(Above) Glasgow's unique Daimler CVD650, D60 of 1951, was almost halfway through its nine-year lifespan when photographed at the St. Enoch Square stance. D60's Alexander body was transferred to D66 (below) in 1960. Alongside is 646, the first of fifteen Weymann-bodied AEC Regent O661s delivered in 1939.

The solitary Mann Egerton body in the fleet had somewhat angular lines, emphasising its 8ft. width and sitting rather awkwardly on the CVD6 chassis of D66 which was of 7ft.6in. wide.

The 'New Look' front on Daimler buses retained some vestige of the exposed radiator by incorporating a fluted motif in the design. One wonders, however, about the lack of exterior radiator filler cap and the inconvenience caused. One of the 1955 Weymann-bodied CVG6 models, D70, is seen at Pollok when quite new, with a Northern Coachbuilders-bodied CVD6 behind. The same cannot be said for the destination screens!

The last batch of 50 Daimler buses for Glasgow — said by some to be the ultimate in rear-platform vehicles — were delivered in 1959. Most were CVG6 models and all had Alexander 61-seat bodywork. D233 is in Renfield Street before the one-way system and British Home Stores had materialised. The GCT Head Office was to the right at this corner with Bath Street.

For the Omnibus Society's Weekend features on D268 such as the Daimler badge and wheel trims were re-fitted and made the vehicle less anonymous than it had been latterly. The smaller fleet numbers were a symptom of the PTE's livery.

(Above) Hawthorn Street at Springburn Road has altered completely since this view was taken in 1960. Passing tram 64 on an enthusiasts' tour, Leyland L46, shows one good reason why the fleet number did not remain under the filler cap for long.

(Left) Ordered in April 1954, the City's first post-war Leylands and the first bought voluntarily since 1937, were 25 of the rare PD2/25 chassis with Pneumocyclic gearbox and 7ft. 6in. overall width. The bodywork, of Weymann design, was built by Alexander. Here L31 emerges from the dark Broomielaw terminus in almost new condition, but already the fitter's light under the canopy is missing although modified cooling grilles for the front brakes have yet to be fitted. The 'pillar of fire' was an early — and potentially lethal — form of traffic bollard.

(Centre) Livery variations on two Coplawhill-bodied Leyland PD2/24 models — also Pneumocyclic but 8ft. wide — which entered service in 1958. L119 (left), seen on Mosspark Boulevard, has no dividing cream band, while the front end of that on L132 (right) is radiussed to correspond with the outline of the cab door window.

(Below) As intended, over 200 forward-entrance buses were used on tram replacement routes and quickly spread to long-established motorbus services. L390, an early example of the PD3/2 batch newly delivered from Alexander's coachworks at Falkirk, shows the entrance area before modifications were made. The painted advert on a new bus is most unusual. In the space originally intended for the BMMO monogram, Glasgow's 'Leyland Albion Titan' badge seems quite at home.

Chapter nine: Post-war Leylands

Although the famous Leyland Titan TD1 had established GCT as one of the country's principal Leyland users, from its introduction in 1928, with further orders for Titans in 1935 and 1937, the post-war versions PD1 and PD2 arrived late in the fleet. A prototype PD2 vehicle (CVA 430) was used on service 2 in 1949, when the rebodied Leylands were returning to service (see *Chapter 4*). Six years later, a PD2/12 type bus (STC 887) was used on the same service. This 8ft. wide example had a Leyland 58-seat body painted in an all-over grey with synchromesh gearbox and traditional exposed radiator. In 1952, the Midland Red company had specified a concealed radiator version with a 'tin front' from Leyland Motors, and this led to the same design being offered to other customers.

GCT ordered 25 Leyland Titans in 1954, and these turned out to be everything demonstrator STC 887 was not. Gone was the traditional radiator, concealed by the 'Midland Red' front. A semi-automatic gearbox using Leyland 'Pneumocyclic' air-operated pedestal control, air brakes and 7ft. 6in. wide body by W. Alexander to MCW Mk I design was specified. No other operators of this PD2/25 combination have been traced, the 8ft. 0in. version being by far the most popular choice. However, L24 was exhibited on W. Alexander's stand at Kelvin Hall, 1955, complete with green trolleybus screens—it seems the coachbuilders did not have any others, as these had been fitted on D67 at Earls Court the previous year. The 60-seat body was steel-framed with aluminium panels and was similar to the 75 Weymann bodies fitted on Daimlers

D68-116 and Regents A315-340. One distinguishing feature was the use of 'jelly-mould' light shades, not found on the English examples. L24-48 were delivered between November 1955 and January 1956.

It will be obvious from the previous chapters that the Department had 'dabbled' in single-deck operation, on a very limited scale, using conventional types—Albion Valkyrie and AEC Regal buses with front entrances (excluding, of course, the initial 1924-28 buses). The two-door arrangement of single-deck Daimlers (DS1-43) and BS1, which was also employed on single-deck trolleybuses, was mainly at the insistence of the General Manager, Mr Fitzpayne, who was strongly influenced by continental practice. A chronic staff shortage plagued GCT throughout the 'fifties and 'sixties. Indeed, in February 1955, Northern Roadways, a large independent company based in the city, offered GCT the use of its vehicles to overcome the difficulties. When it was announced that GCT bus services serving outlying areas such as Johnstone, Paisley, Cambuslang and Clydebank were to be handed over to companies in the Scottish Bus Group, GCT stated that this would release both crews and buses to enable services to new Corporation housing estates to start. With the advent of underfloor-engined single-deckers which permitted a doorway at the extreme front of the bus, one-man-operation became possible and this then seemed an attractive remedy for the continuing shortage of staff. An announcement was made that single-deck one-man operated buses would be operated by

GCT and the Department ordered 30 Leyland chassis; fifteen were to be bodied by W. Alexander and fifteen at the Car Works. This was subsequently changed to 30 MCW-Leyland 'Olympics'.

In 1954, however, a new range of single-deck buses was introduced by Leyland, following on from the underfloored Royal Tiger design. Named 'Royal Tiger Worldmaster', they featured Pneumocyclic gearboxes, air brakes and 8ft. wide 30ft. long chassis. A more powerful O.680 engine could be specified and GCT in fact chose that version although the chassis was, generally speaking, introduced with export orders in mind. The only other British municipal operator to use Worldmasters was Halifax, two years after Glasgow introduced LS1-30 to the fleet. The MCW-Olympic specification meant that no locally-produced bodies could be built, so in order to give local employment, GCT changed the order yet again and purchased 30 Worldmaster chassis and Weymann shells and the bodies were completed at Coplawhill. A separate entrance/exit was called for, with 40 seats and room for standees (continental practice again!). Delivery commenced with LS1-11 in August 1956, LS12-27, 29 in 1957 and LS28 and LS30 in 1958. After being on display at Earls Court in 1956, LS30 was shown on the Leyland stand at Kelvin Hall a year later. In the meantime, conductors were used on the buses in service.

In common with GCT's other experiments in 'continental' and non-conventional passenger flow, the two-door Worldmasters soon proved unpopular and in 1960 a start was made in removing the centre-exit doors, which left a very narrow entrance/exit to cope with embarking and alighting passengers, and four extra seats were fitted. In 1964 the roadway beneath the railway at Hillington Road was lowered and permitted double-deckers to enter Hillington Estate from the south. Services 25 and 40 were converted to double-deck operation and twelve Worldmasters were sold in 1965. The remaining vehicles were used on services 24 and 30 which still required single-deckers. The original intention to operate the Worldmasters without conductors was never carried out as reversing was still required on both remaining services. It was necessary, therefore, to continue to employ conductors to assist at the terminal points.

Back in 1955 when the double-deckers L24-48 were entering service, the technical press had announced that GCT was to purchase a PD2/24 chassis from Leyland with a fully automatic gearbox. This emerged as L49 fitted with an 8ft. wide 60-seat W. Alexander body which made its debut at the demonstration park at the 1956 Earls Court Show. This was said to be the first double-decker to be marketed with an automatic version of the epicyclic transmission and its performance was closely monitored by the technical press and industry. The only clue to the advanced specification was a small electrically-operated switch on the steering column which enabled the fully-automatic transmission to be selected, with positions for neutral and reverse. In March 1957, the bus was subjected to a road test by *Commercial Motor* and the claim made by GCT that an appreciable saving in fuel costs was possible was substantiated. Nevertheless, caution reigned and the following 300 PD2/24 buses ordered had Pneumocyclic semi-automatic gear changes, with air-operated pedestal control. L49 also appeared outside the Kelvin Hall in 1957 — a 'two Show' bus! The traditional rear-entrance arrangement was continued with L50-348 although they seated one more than L49, and all but 100 had W. Alexander bodies of a very similar design to Daimlers D117-267. Coplawhill provided 50 bodies in 1958 and a further 50 in 1960, almost identical to their W. Alexander cousins. L99-123 had hinged doors to the driver's cab while L124-148 and L274-348 had sliding doors. L119 was partially completed by W. Alexander and used by Coplawhill staff as a construction guide. The 1960 batch L324-348 were the last rear platform buses to be built for GCT, the final four being delivered in September 1960.

In 1956 regulations permitted the use of 30ft. long double-deckers with two axles and Leyland introduced a 'stretched' version of the PD2 Titan — designated PD3. Glasgow Corporation was an early convert to

forward-entrance buses and as already seen (*Chapter 6*), had ordered over 200 such buses with W. Alexander bodies seating 72 passengers. As the last rear platform buses emerged from Coplawhill, drivers were delivering the first example of the forward-entrance Titan in July 1960 (L380). These buses were fitted with 'Albion Titan' badges on the tin front, a gesture by Leyland, as Albion could no longer supply the city with double-deckers. They were very much Leyland products, however, and had the same running units as the 27ft. long buses. Coplawhill built L349-374 and delivery was from March 1961-August 1962 — following W. Alexander specification exactly, with no visual difference. St. Helens Corporation had called for a slightly different version of the 'tin front' and this was offered to customers as an optional extra. L398 was designated PD3A/2 (to signify this type of front) and a special interior finish was incorporated for its inclusion at the 1960 Earls Court Show. When City officials inspected the bus with its fluorescent lighting, mushroom-coloured formica panelling, and moquette seats downstairs, no doubt they were impressed. Unfortunately the other 139 buses were of a more spartan finish with green painted metal panels and white enamelled ceilings — the upstairs rapidly turned dark brown(!) — and standard interior GCT/Alexander specification. In addition, few had heaters.

Returning to the single-decker fleet, no sooner had all the Worldmasters been converted to single-door buses, than further discussions took place with the transport unions about one-man-operation. Agreement was eventually reached to operate such buses using a two-door single-deck configuration. GCT, by this time, was firmly wedded to Leyland products and therefore looked to its newly-introduced rear-engined Panther chassis for possible one-man-operation. One was ordered in 1964 and displayed at the 1964 Show. The W. Alexander body displayed continental influence with a 36ft. long front entrance, centre-exit body and room for 42 passengers seated plus a further 31 standing. After delivery from London, LS31 was driven to the North British Locomotive Works in Glasgow, where its semi-automatic Leyland gearbox was replaced by a German-made Voith DIWAbus 200S fully-automatic system. The next few months were occupied by tests in various parts of Glasgow and driver training. By the following spring, agreement was reached to operate the bus without a conductor and service 40 was chosen for the experiment. LS31 entered one-man-operated service on 9th May 1965, with special features including a 'Solomatic' ticket machine, swivelling driver's seat and change-issuing equipment.

After two accidents in seven days, LS31 was withdrawn and returned to the coachbuilders for modifications to the

one-man-operation apparatus. In August it returned to service 21, entering the city centre for the first time in service. A second Panther, LS32, was built for display at the 1965 Kelvin Hall Show and was fitted out similarly to LS31. In February 1966 it also appeared on service 21 but was withdrawn to have a Voith automatic transmission system fitted by May, replacing its Leyland semi-automatic version. The two Panthers were the sole one-man-operated buses for over a year and, as such, needed a back-up vehicle if any withdrawals became necessary. LS26 was chosen and returned to the bus works where an additional exit was fitted (returning the bus to its original condition!) although with seats for 37 passengers compared to 40 previously. As the other OMO single-deckers were painted in the reversed livery, LS26 was outshopped in a similar garb.

By the time the third trial Panther single-decker (LS33) appeared at the 1967 Scottish Show, agreement had been reached nationally and locally to operate double-deckers without conductors and this more or less sealed the fate of GCT's single-deck Panthers. Indeed, the first double-deck OMO Atlantean (LA362) was demonstrated outside Kelvin Hall. LS33 had panorama windows, Voith transmission, SW radio, Bell autoslot machine (coin operated) and luminator lighting. Whilst LS31 and 32 had 18ft. 6in. wheelbases, LS33 had a 17ft. 6in. wheelbase and had the more powerful O.680 engine fitted. Meanwhile, a dispute over OMO limited its use to two vehicles at any one time until further negotiations took place. An order for thirteen further Panthers was placed and in 1969, LS34-42 entered service in February. They were similar to LS33, although with smaller windows. The Voith transmission was dropped in favour of Self Changing Gears' automatic version (LS34 was semi-automatic). By July up to LS45 had been delivered and service 21 could be 100% OMO operated. LS44 and 46 were delayed until December. With the advent of these buses, LS26 was redundant and subsequently with-drawn after little use.

Service 30 was re-routed in March 1970 and was able to be operated by OMO Panthers, the last Worldmasters being used from Maryhill Garage on service 24. On 31st May 1970, this latter route was altered at Gairbraid Avenue and Panthers displaced the 1956-57 buses.

After five trying years of Panther operation, LS31-33 were sold in 1975, the Voith transmission having proved troublesome. However, LS34-46 were not without problems either. The two-door layout was again a source of annoyance to Glasgow passengers who just did not like to leave the vehicle except at the point where they boarded. The engineering staff found the complex system of bell pushes, treadle steps and delay mechanisms did not justify the time spent in repairs and so the centre door was soon isolated and eventually boarded up. The last Panthers, LS35 and 41-46, had the door removed completely and thus seated 45 passengers. One suspects that after years of being informed by irate conductors that they alone were in charge of the 'bells', the Glasgow travellers were most reluctant to pull the cord which set off the complicated chain of events that was required to actually alight at the centre!

By this time the survivors had gathered at Gartcraig for service 30, LS34 had had its electric gearchange replaced by an air-operated pedestal version — just as the Atlanteans were having the reverse carried out. Enough was enough, and in 1977, service 30 was diverted away from the low bridge at South Carntyne and the Panthers were withdrawn. LS35, 41 and 46 underwent an amazing metamorphosis, more of which later ...

The non-Atlantean Leyland fleet was rapidly expiring. Many of the PD3 buses showed signs of their heavy duty on busy tram replacement routes and by 1973 were in need of much rehabilitation. All were withdrawn by May 1976. The rear-entrance buses lingered on until May 1977 when the last (L281, it is generally believed) performed its final duty with little ceremony. Almost 50 years of Titan operation had ended. L108 escaped the scrap yard by virtue of an accident whilst in the driving school fleet in 1976. The top deck was neatly sliced off by a low bridge and the bus was rebuilt to open top figuration. Four seats were removed upstairs some time later, and in 1979 the bus was fitted out downstairs as a mobile exhibition vehicle.

Meanwhile, back at the Bus Works, the three Panthers mentioned previously were being rebuilt as 40-seat coaches. LS46 was first tackled in 1977, completed by December and numbered

C2. The floor level was raised, thus providing some luggage space on the nearside and inside at the rear. Coach trim consisted of parcel racks, weathershield rooflights, and padded coach bulkheads. The multi-windows from its bus days were replaced by standard Atlantean panoramic glasses. The vehicles retained the bus style

windscreen. C3 and C4 were completed by the summer of 1978, basically similar, but with provision for a small destination display in the front 'dome'. The coaches were used on the City Tour and helped build up a demand for private hire vehicles until 1981 when they were sold, sufficient new coaches having been delivered by then.

L99-148 had GCT bodies to W. Alexander design. L24-48 had PD2/25 chassis.
LS1-30 had RT3/1 chassis, L49-348 were PD2/24s, L349-97/9-488 were PD3/2s, L398 was PD3A/2, LS31-33 were PSUR1/1R chassis and LS34-46 were PSUR1A/1R.
LS34-46 had seating for 43 passengers.
Registrations: L24-48 were FYS 647-671, L49-98 were FYS 877-926, L99-248 were SGD 1-150, L249-488 were SGD 251-490, LS1-30 were FYS 672-700, 876. LS31 was CYS 139B, LS32 was GYS 878D, LS33 was NUS 834F and LS34-46 were PYS 987-999G.
The reversed livery was applied to: L31, 144, 175, 233, 238, 277-9.
L241, 257-261, 263-7, 287 were converted to works vehicles.
The following were used as Learner buses after passenger service:-
L24, 27-31, 33, 37-9, 41, 44-6, 50-61, 63, 108, 177, 187, 247, 256, 280, 284, 288, 290-2, 268, 270-1, 319, 325-8, 346.

(Above) After trials with three of the rear-engined Leyland Panthers, a batch of thirteen with Alexander bodywork was delivered in 1969. This unlucky 'bakers dozen' were neither particularly reliable nor popular. With the reversed livery, it was thought unnecessary to inform the passenger of one-man operation. The GCT bus stops had not changed radically since the earliest days and the design shown beside LS34 was also adopted by Clydebank Burgh for Central SMT services within its boundaries — with the appropriate letters — BOC.

As a stop-gap, three Panthers had considerable work carried out for further use as coaches, although retaining traces of their original condition. Only two other buses in the Department's long history carried '999' registrations — D217 and A119 (Volvo). C2 (ex LS46) was at a wet Ballochmyle Hospital in Ayrshire when photographed on an enthusiasts' tour. No destination screens were fitted to this rebuild.

When the Leyland Atlantean, which introduced the rear-engined double-decker to the British urban transport scene, was developed only a few city tram fleets in the country remained to be scrapped or closed down. In Sheffield, its trams survived long enough for Atlanteans to operate briefly alongside them but only in Glasgow could this scene have taken place until as late as 1962. Curiously, Scotland's only other Atlanteans (with MCW bodies) in existence at that time could have been similarly photographed — being with the fleet of Laurie of Hamilton and, latterly, taken over by Central SMT. 'Coronation' tram 1291 is reflected on an advert-free LA1 in Hope Street soon after delivery in 1958. Alexander's initial interpretation of a body design for the model was less severe than the MCW version on other early examples but gave only a hint of what was to follow.

The 'Glasgow Style' W. Alexander body, first seen in 1962, incorporated curved windscreens derived from those of this bodybuilder's Y-type single-decker and generously domed roof panels; it was soon to be featured in fleets throughout the country. LA2 displays its now familiar lines at Hillington. The railway bridge remained a barrier for double-deckers entering Hillington Estate from the south until 1964 when it was rebuilt. The work is proceeding in the background. Half of the unique front cream band on LA2 has already succumbed to the painter's brush.

At one time, the stage carriage licences held by the SCWS in south-west Glasgow were operated by Smith's of Barrhead and one such service covered South Nitshill where LA186 met the latter's RGA 632 in 1968. The green and cream lowbridge body on the Leyland Titan contrasts sharply with Glasgow's 'Standard' vehicle despite there being only six years between designs.

With its Self Changing Gears fully-automatic gearbox, Atlantean LA362 was Glasgow's first double-deck bus to be fitted out for one-man operation. It is pictured outside Kelvin Hall acting as a demonstration vehicle at the 1967 Scottish Motor Show.

More than a decade apart...Eleven years separated the entry into service of these two vehicles. Coplawhill-bodied Leyland PD2 L108 is seen with LA475, one of 35 dual-doorway Atlanteans of 1969. Although the orange dot on the dome was supposed to signify a one-man operated vehicle, there was unfortunately no means of covering this up if a conductor was on board. L108 survives as an open-topper.

50

Prototype Glasgow Corporation Atlantean LA1 was set aside for preservation and can now be seen at the Kelvin Hall Museum of Transport alongside Albion B92 and trolleybus TBS13. The original side lights have been altered, the Glasgow 'Albion' badge has replaced the first design and a later engine cover arrangement fitted.

Chapter ten: The Leyland Atlanteans

'Glasgow Corporation to operate 86-passenger bus from January 1957'. Such a headline in today's passenger transport press would hardly raise an eyebrow, but when readers of *Motor Transport* were greeted with this news in August 1956, the impact that the Atlantean bus would have on road transport throughout the UK could hardly have been foreseen.

The conception of this revolutionary vehicle has been well documented elsewhere. Suffice to say that the prototype bus 281 ATC was exhibited at the 1956 Earls Court Show and immediately afterwards began a tour of operators for demonstration work. It entered service with Ribble Motor Services in October 1956 from Bootle Garage for two weeks' trial. If the headlines mentioned above are to be believed, then GCT had plans to use the bus in service, but, in the event, 281 ATC was only inspected by officials of the Department and Corporation.

A production version of the Atlantean with conventional suspension, the PDR1/1, was developed and several buses were ready for exhibition at the 1958 Show. Four complete Atlanteans were in attendance: Wallasey Corporation No. 1 (FHF 451), James of Ammanford No. 227 (RTH 637), Maidstone & District No. DL43 (43 DKT) and GCT No. LA1. The first three had bodies from the MCW group but Glasgow's bus was bodied by W. Alexander (Coachbuilders). This was the first instance that the Scottish bodybuilder had exhibited its products in London under the Company's own name, and in common with normal W. Alexander practice, LA1 did not display a registration number. The coachbuilders had recently moved from Stirling to a new factory at Falkirk and LA1 was the first bus to be completed at this location. Delivery to GCT took place on 26th November whereupon the bus was registered FYS 998. The first production Atlantean to go into service was actually Wallasey No. 1, having beaten LA1 by just a few days. GCT's first Atlantean was sent to Ibrox Garage and began work on 15th December 1958 on service 4.

Although the W. Alexander examples for Glasgow (and, later, Newcastle, Belfast and Gateshead & District) were slightly different from the MCW design, they were regarded by many as being too 'box-like' with very shallow top deck windows and flat, upright fronts. The rear engine bustle was an immediate give-away as to the position of the power unit and no attempt was made to disguise it. Glasgow officials later inspected Liverpool Corporation's E2 (372 BKA) which was of similar appearance and they expressed their disapproval of the appearance of these buses. Work was undertaken to improve the design of rear-engined bus bodies and, in a joint effort with W. Alexander (Coachbuilders), Glasgow Corporation Transport produced a double-deck body with wrap-round windscreens, and rounded front and rear domes. This design, soon labelled 'Glasgow Style', was introduced in 1962 and not only became popular throughout the country but was imitated by other builders and set the pattern for future W. Alexander designs, which were produced until 1984. LA4 was the first 'Glasgow' Atlantean, delivered on 17th August 1962, and this event commenced a non-stop delivery run of nearly 20 years' purchases amounting to 1,448 buses — the world's largest Atlantean fleet for one operator. This number accounts for nearly one third of the total buses operated by GCT and its successors from 1924-1984! Such a vast number of buses deserves closer scrutiny!

If LA2 and LA1449 were examined side by side, there could be no doubt that the latter was the modern-day equivalent of the former. Despite the years between them, many features were to be found on both buses and, generally, could be called the post-war standard buses, if only because of the sheer volume built. Having said that, although LA2 and LA1449 were undoubtedly from the same manufacturers, they were worlds' apart as far as passenger comfort, driving controls and mechanical features were concerned. How then, were these changes achieved during the long production? It is perhaps best to consider the batches in chronological order, noting the more interesting changes that occurred. The Atlantean introduced to the fleet fluorescent lighting (except LA1) and saloon heaters on a regular basis, but the use of front entrance doors had already been established by the 229 Leyland Titans and AEC Regents already in service, and, of course, the single-deckers previously described.

LA2 — 102. Delivered August 1962 — December 1962 (101). These buses were in time for the last tram replacement service (64) but soon spread to other routes. The chassis were to Mk II specification, with O.600 semi-Power Plus engines, fluid-friction couplings and Pneumocyclic gearboxes with electric gearchange on steering column. Leyland Motors had chosen Atlas, portrayed as supporter of the world, for the Atlantean badge, but A(t)las he did not appear on GCT's fleet. A special Leyland-Albion Atlantean badge was designed which made use of the St. Andrew's Cross for Glasgow's buses and LA2 — 600 had these fitted. On some occasions, chassis intended for Glasgow but diverted to other customers had the same badge. The Glasgow style bodywork which was 8in. longer than the previously permitted 30ft. 0in. encouraged other operators to take some GCT vehicles for periods of demonstration. LA6 went to Coventry, LA83 to Birkenhead, LA138 to CIE, Ireland (just three examples) and, eventually, Leyland bought LA91 in April 1963 to continue this work. LA2 had the cream band extended round the front of the bus when new. The heater intake for these buses was under the rear canopy. Non-nicotine staining white plastic ceiling panels were introduced in both saloons in these buses as first used on L398 and A351. These were subject to rippling and de-lamination quite soon and, on a few buses, had to be replaced by painted aluminium — although **not** always the entire ceiling had to be so treated!

LA103 — 202. Delivered September 1963 — March 1964 (100). There was no change from the previous batch other than the employment of an additional interior light on the rear dome upstairs and the repositioning of the heater intakes to either side of the rear registration plate, to avoid short circuiting of exhaust fumes into the heating system. Halfway through the batch, the detailing of interior advertising frames was amended. Some buses reverted to painted aluminium interior roof panels following a fire at the plastics shop at W. Alexander's factory. One Atlantean from this batch outlived the others. LA184 was used as a shop stewards' office from 1976-81. The engine and auxiliary equipment was removed.

LA203 — 284. Delivered October 1964-May 1965 (82). The last bus of this batch was fitted with external illuminating advert panels lit from concealed lower saloon lighting, being exhibited at the International Transport Exhibition at Munich in 1965 before entering service. The interior lower saloon floor was ramped, rather than stepped at the rear axle. In December 1970, LA284 was used on a newly-introduced Centre Circle (200) with the illuminated exterior panels on both sides and other advertising space reserved for a city centre butcher. The illuminated advert panels were removed late in 1973 before the bus was painted in 'Busy Bee' livery. Also in that year, LA243 was converted to an open-topper after an accident. However, it was never used in this condition and quickly received a new roof.

This batch also saw the introduction of glass fibre bumpers surrounding the base of the engine compartment, and this was added to earlier buses also. In order to train mechanics, LA253's chassis was retained at the works until 1986. Each component was easily identified as *in situ*.

LA285 — 321. Delivered September 1965 — April 1966 (37).

LA322. Delivered November 1966 (1). This was Glasgow's first Atlantean to have a fully automatic gearbox made by Voith, and also had non-standard interior trim, featuring glass fibre seats upstairs and curved-back grey and green leathercloth covered seats downstairs. After three years out of use, the transmission was replaced by a conventional semi-automatic gearbox and the bus returned to service in 1974.

LA323 — 364. Delivered January 1967 — April 1967 (42). Several of this batch had ramped floors, i.e. LA335-339, 341-364. LA362 had its normal gearbox replaced by an SCG fully automatic gearbox in July 1967 and was converted to one-man-operation, with features deemed necessary including reversing lights (ex-AEC Regent headlamps!), a

periscope for upper deck surveillance and bracket for ticket machine and money tray fitted near driver's cabin. It was used as a demonstrator outside the Kelvin Hall at the 1967 Scottish Motor Show.

LA365 — 421. Delivered August 1967 — February 1968 (57). First major change to interior design with Formica panelling (green), sliding windows (replacing hopper ones), curved seats backs, ramped floors and one-piece rear top-deck emergency window. The chassis had the more powerful O.680 engine and gear change was effected by an air-operated floor mounted pedestal gear knob (as supplied on GCT Titans). LA399 was on show at Millburn Motors in November 1967, and afterwards fitted with 'Luminator' interior lighting which provided space for adverts along the interior sides of the bus.

LA422. Delivered July 1968 (1). This was another 'one-off' bus, built to the new maximum width of 8ft. 2½in., and the first dual-doored Atlantean, with forward ascending stair and fully automatic gearbox. It entered service from Newlands Garage on service 21 (Pollok-Midland Street) alongside omo Panthers and LA362 on 1st November 1968.

LA423 — 464, 466 — 499. Delivered August 1968 — July 1969 (76). This batch was split into single doorway version (LA423-464) and 2-door buses (LA466-499), which were also 8ft. 2½in. wide. LA466-481 had passenger-operated ticket machines fitted on nearside bulkhead, reducing the seating capacity by one, and introduced on service 28 (Milton-Renfrew Street) in February 1970. All machines were removed by summer 1973, after falling out of use. LA451-464, 466-500 had fibre glass seats on top deck. Number LA474 had a passenger counter fitted when new. LA472-499 had 'Luminator' interior lighting. LA464 (only) had previous style of upper-deck emergency door used on LA2-364 (split windows). Fibre glass seating proved unpopular with passengers and was removed on some buses to be replaced with conventional seating (7ft. 6in. width-style) displaced from withdrawn vehicles.

LA465. Delivered January 1970 (1). It was exhibited at the 1969 Motor Show, Glasgow, and had 'Luminator' lighting, passenger counter and special interior trim. It entered service in May 1970, with fully auto gearbox and, to conform to new psv regulations, windscreen washers.

LA500. Delivered October 1969 (1). 'Luminator' lighting fitted.

LA501 — 550. Delivered June 1970 — January 1971 (50). Introduced revised style for dash panel

1972-built LA603 demonstrates the re-designed front end and electric gearchange on the steering column introduced from LA501 onwards. Although still wearing Glasgow Corporation Transport's final livery, the lack of a crest and revised legal lettering indicates that ownership has passed to the Greater Glasgow PTE.

The lower deck of LA422, Glasgow's first dual-doorway Alexander-bodied Leyland Atlantean, represented the Corporation Transport Department's 'swansong' as far as passenger comfort was concerned. The bell pull cord was a curious revival, briefly returning to favour in various fleets, although a feature of GCT buses for many years.

and returned to electric gearchange on steering column, which was eventually fitted to earlier air-operated gearchange buses, power steering and parking brake. All fitted with radio, one-man-operated layout and 'Luminator' lighting. Due to the tendency to cause flat batteries at terminal points, half the lighting tubes were disconnected, then removed completely in 1974-77, being replaced by standard GCT lighting. The 'Luminator' lighting was intended to display advertisement transparencies but, other than on LA465 especially equipped for its Motor Show appearance, no buses are believed to have used this provision to advantage in service. LA521 had a plastic lower saloon emergency door. LA524 had an experimental split windscreen.

LA551—600. Delivered September 1971—April 1972 (50). 'Luminator' lighting fitted when new and subsequently replaced as above. LA589

retained full 'Luminator' display, until removal of this equipment. Batch had split windscreens and radios fitted as standard. LA574 was exhibited at the 1971 Kelvin Hall Show and had minor differences including recessed fluorescent cab light, and anti-vandal alarm (which became standard equipment). LA599 and LA600 had automatic gearboxes fitted, the former of Lucas CAV type and the latter Self Changing Gears. In 1974 a start was made to remove the centre-exit doors from those buses so equipped. Two Atlanteans, LA559 and LA736, were the prototypes dealt with and the centre door and bulkheads were removed completely, thus giving 31 seats downstairs. 'Home-made' Luminator lighting was installed where the exit doors had been! A further conversion (LA570) had the middle door overpanelled and a pram pen built into the space between the exit bulkheads as an interim measure. This gave 27

seats in the lower saloon. However, a bench seat for two people was fitted in this area, a window fitted and doors removed by 1975. Work then commenced on modifying all the two-door buses in passenger service and this was completed by 1979. The 'production' conversions retained the interior bulkheads in the process, seating 29 downstairs. Buses not dealt with were thus suitable for trainer vehicles using the centre door. It is believed that LA710 was reconverted to this learner vehicle layout and the front door was removed.

LA601—750. Delivered November 1972—December 1973 (150). Introduced new W. Alexander aluminium-framed 'AL' body with flat roofs, equal depth windows on both decks and conventional interior lighting. Two-door layout continued. From the start of this batch, Atlanteans had Brunswick green wheels and black

53

Grüsse aus Schottland
von den Glasgower Bürgern
an die Hamburger Bürger

The GGPTE's logo was first applied to LA751 at the Kelvin Hall show in 1973 and four months later it travelled to Hamburg to represent the City. Extra attention was given to details such as wheel rings (from Edinburgh), a coat of varnish, a 'GB' plate and a City Coat of Arms.

Eight Atlanteans were rebuilt to single-deckers and are reminiscent of the Marshall-bodied Fleetlines that Birmingham City Transport purchased in 1965. SA1 has since been repainted in an all-over advertising livery; it had played a similar role when a double-decker, LA850, a decade earlier.

On occasions the weather allows City Tour passengers to brave the elements on one of the two Atlanteans so converted. LA957 sports the 1980-84 tour livery plus Trans-Clyde logo as it loads up at St. Enoch Square. The public address system would appear to be lost to upper deck visitors.

LA1024 would probably not have been used on Glasgow's tours, but once it had left the fleet a similar new life for it was found by a York operator. It is seen in the Stonebow which lies within York's historic City Walls.

bumpers, a painting style which subsequently spread to rest of fleet. Leyland Motors introduced revised Atlantean chassis AN68/1 in early 1972. This changed the coding system, with 'Radalarm' warning system added; improved final drive mechanism; power steering; three part engine cover with hinged end panels (which incorporated additional air intakes) and air-operated gear change—although Glasgow opted for the electric switch on steering column, and provision on the chassis for wider passenger entrance/exits and revised driving controls. All had one-piece windscreens except LA614, 615, 618, 619, 620, 634-645, 712 onwards, which had split screens. LA630 was test bus for fitting of anti-vandal drivers' screen to cab door in May 1975; this was subsequently fitted to all Atlanteans. LA637 was used as experimental Almex fare collection bus for trials before adopting this system. In July 1973, LA644 was destroyed after a fire but subsequently rebodied by W. Alexander later that year with post-'750' standard design. LA691 onwards had engine shrouds fitted. These were the first buses to have reflective registration plates front and rear. LA714 featured experimental interior trim with the green Formica panels restricted to below window ledges and white being employed above this, as later appeared from LA801 upwards.

LA751—825. Delivered December 1973—June 1974 (75). LA751 introduced new standard PTE body, influenced by the first PTE Director General, Mr R. Cox, with panoramic windows, one door layout, revised destination layout, Edinburgh-style interior lights, as on AV1-3, light green interior and seats, and a luggage rack on nearside. Shown at the 1973 Kelvin Hall exhibition, it introduced 'GG' symbols and white or yellow reflective fleet plates. In March 1974 the bus took part in a Glasgow Week at Hamburg and carried passengers in that city, finally entering service in November 1974. LA752-800 had interiors similar to pre-750 batches, 801 upwards had '750' type interior, but 'Glasgow' lights. LA806 had G2 auto-gearbox fitted when new. Internal 'Please Pay Driver' boards, illuminated from destination box, were fitted to LA751-1310. These were reversible when used on conductor-operated services and removed later when all services were omo. LA795 was chosen to have smaller windows fitted on the lower deck. *See below.*

LA826—850. Delivered August 1974—October 1974 (25). It was the discovery of serious body defects on the panoramic-windowed Atlanteans in 1981 that led to the premature withdrawal of many from the LA800-1050 range. Some survivors had modifications carried out either at W. Alexander's premises or at the Bus Works. LA850 was chosen to be

converted to a single-decker and was the first example to be completed by Spring 1982 into a 31-seater for use in the inter-station service, (SA1). Buses LA751-800 originally only had one lower saloon off-side sliding ventilator. This was increased to two, conforming with later vehicles quite soon.

LA851—1050. Delivered November 1974—June 1976 (200). LA871 was converted to single-deck SA4. LA881 was fitted when new with one piece destination aperture, removed later. LA901 upwards introduced right-hand gear change, first fitted on LA751. LA906-15 had CAV auto-transmission when new. LA918 and 938 became SA7 and 8 respectively. LA930 was converted to single-decker SA2. LA944-5 had prototype large Young's hopper window vents. LA957 was converted to open-topper early 1978 after an accident. LA962 was rebuilt as SA3. LA966 upwards had AN68A/IR chassis with Leyland National type 5-speed semi-auto gearchange. LA975 was converted in 1982 to survey staff bus with calor gas lighting, toilet facilities, eating accommodation, and office space. By late 1984, it had been repainted in standard livery and converted into an exhibition bus. LA979 was rebuilt as SA5. LA987 was exhibited at 1975 Kelvin Hall Show as 'LA1000'. Subsequently renumbered LA1000 after entering service. At a special ceremony, BL Chairman, Lord Stokes, unveiled a plaque to commemorate the addition of the 1000th Atlantean to Glasgow's fleet. The plaque was removed from the bus soon after! LA1028 had non-standard vents fitted above front windscreen.

LA1051—1100. Delivered August 1976—December 1976 (50). A revised windscreen wiper arrangement was introduced from LA1090. Some buses from the earlier part of this batch had protruding fog lights which must have been very susceptible to damage if a driver edged too close to the bus in front when boarding passengers. Normal dash panels were soon fitted with recessed lights.

LA1101—1250. Delivered February 1977—June 1978 (150). Hopper windows (as LA944-5) and 'Cronapress' bell fittings were introduced from LA1101, replacing long-familiar cords! LA 1140 had fold-down front dash panel, fitted also to LA1151-1175. LA1117 converted to single-decker SA6. LA1151 upwards introduced additional two seats on bottom deck by fitting back-to-back seats over rear wheel arches. LA1165 reverted to dark green seating and this became standard again. LA1215 and 1217 were used for Almex and autofare trials respectively before entering service. LA1220 was damaged by a low bridge and converted to open-top by April 1978.

LA1251—1310. Delivered January 1979—May 1979 (60). Introduced 'high-drive' cab layout featuring a higher driving position and deeper offside cab window which is out of line with top of lower deck windows. LA1275-1280 had Firestone H.E.L.P. energy absorbing bumpers. LA1295 was used for livery and interior design experiments before entering service.

LA1311—1350. Delivered October 1979—January 1980 (40). Introduced a revised destination screen layout with a one-piece aperture (as LA881 originally) which incorporated an off-side service number; external illuminated omo sign (which originally had 'Conductor operated' or 'Pay As You Enter' legend); fold-down dash panels and revised heater arrangements with air intake on the offside, behind the driver's window. The rear heater intakes under the canopy were no longer required and discontinued.

This brings the Atlantean deliveries up to January 1980, including 600 large-windowed bodies in use, most of which had shown some signs of deterioration due to the flexing action of the Atlantean chassis coupled with one-door W. Alexander bodies. Unlike other operators' specifications, these did not have the strengthening effect of dual entrance and exits. Modifications were carried out to reinforce the side frames where possible. To gain experience and evaluate the results of such alterations, two fully laden (with weights!) Atlanteans (LA1324 and LA1330) were used in full 'Reserved' daily service running to a timetable. The panoramic windows were removed from the lower deck and substituted by small bay type size glass. Number LA1330 has three small windows on the nearside, and five on the offside. It was decided that such a campaign would have been too time consuming and costly and, as a result, many buses were withdrawn after only a short period of service. LA1180 was converted to small lower deck windows also.

LA1351—1439. Delivered August 1980—December 1980 (89). This batch marked a return to short bay bodies of a much superior specification—believed by many to be the best W. Alexander-bodied products to date, with up-market interiors which called for moquette seating on both decks (similar to the Underground pattern), two piece glider entrance doors, illuminated exterior 'omo' sign, ribbed floors on both decks, two-step entrance, large destination aperture with offside service number and provision for two single line destination displays, light brown and black interior decor, with white satin finished ceilings. LA1351-62, 1364 had patterned ceilings on both decks, but due to de-lamination problems, a start was made in replacing this in late 1984 with plain white finish. The provision for showing a 'via' display below main destination was not used. At first, the single screen was used on the top, lower aperture blanked off. Following complaints from traffic staff, who found difficulty in setting the top screen correctly (when viewed from inside the bus) the lower position was used. When it became obvious that no agreement could be reached in the use of two screens incorporating 'via' points, most buses had the entire box altered to show a one-line destination alongside the triple track service number box. LA1393, LA1406 and LA1421 have not been converted. LA1436 and 1437 were chosen to be converted to accept wheelchairs and had an access ramp fitted to the rear of the front axle. Seating in these buses was reduced to fifteen in the lower deck to permit three wheelchairs. The moquette seating was removed downstairs at this time and the remaining seats were of the black vinyl variety. On the wheelchair vehicles, the omo sign has been removed from the front dash. LA1430 had large destination window, replaced by single aperture as seen on LA1311-1350 batch, after accident damage. After severe accident damage, late in 1985, LA1401 and LA1431 were both dismantled at the Works.

LA1440, 1443, 1449. Delivered April 1981 (3). One of these buses was chosen for conversion to wheelchair carriage—LA1440.

LA1441, 1442, 1444-8. Delivered 25th September 1981 (7). These were the last deliveries of Atlanteans for Glasgow with semi-automatic gearboxes as opposed to the automatic versions which had been specified in later years. In some records they are therefore assigned the chassis code AN68/1R. LA1442 was converted for wheelchair use.

Thought was given in 1982-83 to providing a larger number screen display on those Atlanteans which had the larger destination window (LA1351-1449, except LA1430). This was to bring them into line with the other types of buses bought in recent years. However, the idea was dropped until 1986 when LA1111 was modified to assess this change. Plans to convert the last batch of Atlantean to Voith transmission with Cummins engines did not come to fruition, due, it is believed, to the difficulty of fitting this equipment into the limited space available at the rear of the bus.

Chassis types:- PDR1/1 — LA1-500; PDR1A/1 — LA501-600; AN68/1R — LA601-965; AN68A/1R — LA966-1449.
Seating Capacity:- 78 seats — LA1-421, 423-464, 1151-1449.
75 seats — LA422, 465-850. 31 seats — SA1-6. 35 seats — SA7-8.
76 seats — LA851-1150.
Registrations:-

LA1	FYS 998	LA951-986	KSU 827-862P
LA2-161	SGD 580-740	LA987	KSU 876P
LA162-221	AGA 101-160B	LA988-999	KSU 864-875P
LA222-242	CYS 568-588B	LA1000	KSU 863P
LA243-302	DGE 280-339C	LA1001-1050	MDS 664-713P
LA303-320	GYS 879-896D	LA1051-1100	RUS 302-351R
LA321-364	KUS 576-619E	LA1101-1120	TGE 820-839R
LA365-414	MUS 250-299F	LA1121-1150	TGG 736-765R
LA415-421	NUS 835-841F	LA1151-1185	UGG 370-404R
LA422-458	PYS 950-986G	LA1186-1188	WUS 579-581S
LA459-508	UGA 212-261H	LA1189-1200	WUS 567-578S
LA509-550	XGA 7-48J	LA1201-1250	XUS 572-621S
LA551-600	BGA 509-558K	LA1251-1310	FSU 68-127T
LA601-650	FUS 121-170L	LA1311-1350	LSU 368-407V
LA651-710	HGD 857-916L	LA1351-1360	RDS 565-574W
LA711-760	NGB 79-128M	LA1361-1385	RDS 540-564W
LA761-810	OYS 158-207M	LA1386-1429	RDS 575-618W
LA811-825	RGB 592-606M	LA1430-1439	SUS 598-607W
LA826-850	SGA 709-733N	LA1440	UGB 193W
LA851-867	GGG 303-319N	LA1441-2	CUS 296-7X
LA868-892	GNS 660-684N	LA1443	UGB 196W
LA893-900	HGG 242-249N	LA1444-5	UGB 197-8W
LA901-925	JGA 183-207N	LA1446-8	CUS 300-2X
LA926-950	JUS 773-797N	LA1449	UGB 202W

The following buses were painted in the reversed livery:- LA24, 27, 188.
LA1, 14, 20, 45, 49, 50, 105, 107, 109, 110, 117, 130, 150, 152, 161, 174, 191-2, 196, 198, 201, 220, 225, 227, 230, 236, 254, 258-9, 263, 265, 267, 270, 273, 279, 282, 287-8, 290, 294-9, 301, 303-4, 308, 318, 354, 367, 479-80, 489, 611-3, 615, 680-682, 684, 695, 697-700, 710, 713-4, 717-20, 728, 730, 735, 737-8,
741-2, 745, 761, 785, 810, 812 were all used as Learner buses after passenger service.

Four Alexander-bodied Leyland Atlanteans, LA1436/7, 1440/2, were converted at Larkfield Bus Works to carry wheelchair passengers for use in normal service with an attendant. LA1442 was one of the final batch delivered in 1981, bringing to an end almost two decades of continuous purchases of this chassis/body combination.

In May 1974, the Presidential visit of the Omnibus Society included a display of vehicles at Larkfield Works, where several vehicles were inspected. Metropolitan M1 entered service some six months in advance of the others and is framed between NVP 533M, the prototype Metropolitan (right) and a Leyland National demonstrator (left). The 'Please Pay Driver' sign, whose origin was likely to have been with the Tyne and Wear PTE, and the exposed radio aerial were standard features married to the MCW specification.

Chapter eleven: The Metropolitans: an unfortunate stop gap

Because of considerable dissatisfaction with existing rear-engined products and their apparent inherent unreliability, the Metropolitan was born. This vehicle was the result of joint development work between the Swedish Scania-Vabis company and Metro-Cammell. A new design of bus which would use Swedish mechanical components married to MCW-built bodywork, would, it was hoped, iron out the deficiencies of the existing range of buses and provide a quieter and more comfortable vehicle for the passenger. While the engine remained at the rear, it was 'encapsulated' in its own box to ensure proper cooling and operational conditions. The air intake was placed on the roof with the radiator mounted forward of the rear axle. Much of the design was derived from the existing Metro-Scania single-decker and, in turn, Scania's own models.

With this promise in mind, the Department in May 1972 ordered twenty such vehicles—right off the drawing board! It was no secret that the availability of spare parts and gearboxes for Atlanteans was causing concern and indeed threats were made to cancel future orders from Leyland if the position did not improve. A prototype double-decker, NVP 533M with two-door layout, was at the Kelvin Hall in 1973 as a demonstrator. This bus returned briefly to Glasgow in May 1974 for a display of vehicles held at Larkfield Works in connection with the Omnibus Society's Presidential Weekend.

The first of this £278,360 order was delivered in May 1974—M1 was the first non-Alexander-bodied (or -inspired) double-decker since 1955! Glasgow's 'fling' with two-door Leyland Atlanteans was at an end, and, following the current practice, only one entrance/exit was provided. Despite being the largest buses operated up till then (31ft. 10in. long by 8ft. 2½in. wide), the seating capacity was limited to 73, due largely to the engine compartment at the rear encroaching

into the lower saloon. As there was no 'bustle', a large shelf inside the rear of the lower saloon gave the impression of much wasted space.

After having trained sufficient drivers to work the Metropolitans, the management placed M1 on one-man-operated service 53 from Possilpark Garage in August 1974. The air suspension provided a very wallowy ride and, being driven in the usual Glasgow manner, did not endear the bus to older passengers. Neither did the step mid-way along the lower saloon floor which caused many a parcel-laden passenger to assume a horizontal position without warning! Nothing daunted, the remainder, M2-20, were delivered by January 1975. M4 was displayed at Earls Court and earned itself a special stainless steel GG symbol on the front dash (which was removed rather quickly once the bus was in Glasgow), and flush-panelled light covers. The interior followed closely the standard W. Alexander/PTE decor with light green seats and white and green surfaces. M21-40 followed in May, having been ordered late in 1974.

With their powerful 11-litre engine and automatic transmission, the buses soon proved themselves to be troublesome in wet or icy road conditions. Bad driving was an obvious factor but, nevertheless, braking and air suspension problems also began to take their toll of serviceable buses. The fuel consumption was very high in comparison with their GCT stablemates. Spare parts from Sweden also raised many an eyebrow when invoices were sent! The batch was split initially between Possilpark and Bridgeton Garages, ensuring to a certain extent that at least one service (18—Burnside or Shawfield and Springburn) was

operated by these powerful buses. In 1976, when Argyle Street services were re-routed via Queen, Ingram and Stockwell Streets, away from the excavations in conjunction with the building of the Argyle Street railway station on the Central low-level line, all services except the 18 had time added to their schedules, to take account of this. The Metropolitans had ample reserves to cope with delays thus caused!

When Bridgeton Garage closed, the Metropolitans were moved to Partick and in due course to Newlands Garage. These nomadic buses appeared to be unwanted and unloved. As if to vindicate their purchase, however, M33 was 'allowed' to take part in the Open Day procession in 1978. A more serious situation arose when the vehicles approached their first major overhaul. Much corrosion and rusting of the steel framework had taken place and this fact hastened their demise from the fleet. Many languished out of use for some time before being sold, and the rest of the serviceable buses were allocated to Possilpark. None was repainted in subsequent PTE liveries (*Chapter 15*) and the last was delicensed in July 1982. At least one (M31) survived long enough to operate one of the services extended outwith the City after the removal of the inherited monopoly of bus routes in 1982 and was noted in service going to Auchinairn on the 37 route on 8th April that year.

The stop-gap between the original rear-engined double-deckers and future designs had been less successful than hoped as far as Glasgow was concerned. Perhaps the new generation which was emerging would prove to be better, although a re-think in the position of the engine was deemed to be necessary. Read on ....

Metropolitans M1-40 had Scania BR111DH chassis and were registered:-
M1 RGA 304M; M2-20 GGA 56-74N; M21-40 JUS 741-760N

Lying south of Castlemilk is the village of Carmunnock, serviced by Glasgow Corporation Transport and its successors since the Young's take over in 1941. The driver of the third pre-production Ailsa double-decker, AV3, has already changed the destination as it nears the rural terminus. AV1-3 of 1975 were the only buses with front and rear peaked domes in the fleet, though Alexander had tended to favour the style as part of its new generation body design family of the early 'seventies. Barely visible here are the panoramic side windows specified to conform with the style on GGPTE Atlanteans.

Chapter twelve: the new generation

At the same time as Scania was pinning its hopes on entering the British psv market, other manufacturers were thinking along the same lines. The Ailsa concern, based at Barrhead, about seven miles from Glasgow, then primarily Volvo's British truck and bus agency, had given the matter of rear-engined bus chassis a great deal of thought. With the Scottish Bus Group voicing its opinion of the then current models available, the opportunity was ripe for co-operation between Ailsa and the SBG. This resulted in the production of a front-engined bus chassis which would still be suitable for one-man-operation and, more importantly, qualify for the Government's bus grant. The front-engined chassis had been normal since the earliest buses produced, with few deviations along the way, particularly with double-deckers. Ailsa saw this configuration as a more suitable design for heavy duty city work, rather than persevering with the problems inherent in the rear-engined variety. Volvo decided to build a new factory at Irvine, Ayrshire, where production of the new bus chassis, AB57, would commence.

Close consulation had also been maintained with W. Alexander (Coachbuilders) and this resulted in the prototype Ailsa having a 79-seat body built at Falkirk. THS 273M was exhibited at the 1973 Kelvin Hall Show, painted in Alexander (Midland) blue

and cream livery. It was used by Midland in March 1974, followed by demonstration work throughout Scotland, including Glasgow (evidently avoiding the problems which beset the Guy Wulfrunian over a decade previously) in August. A pre-production run of ten vehicles was started and these went to PTEs in Greater Glasgow (3), West Yorkshire (1), the West Midlands (3) and Tyne and Wear (3). Glasgow's first Ailsa-Volvo AV1 was finished in time for Earls Court 1974. Whereas THS 273M had a multi-windowed body, AV1 was built using the then standard GGPTE specification of panoramic windows, but retaining the peak domes of the prototype. A Volvo 6.7-litre turbocharged engine provided the power via a Self Changing Gears automatic gearbox, with power steering as standard fitment. A Show 'refinement' was the use of Edinburgh-style light covers (also fitted on LA751). AV1 entered service from Larkfield in March 1974 on service 31/31A, followed two months later by AV2 and 3, which also had non-standard interior lighting. AV1 and 3 also sported electrically-heated windscreens, a rare refinement for Glasgow.

Fifteen production AB57 chassis were ordered by the PTE and delivery was made late in 1975 (AV4-18). The peak domes were replaced by standard Atlantean designs although panoramic windows were continued, thus making

them more akin to the rest of the fleet. Interior lighting was to the PTE's (formerly GCT's) standard fitment. AV11 was demonstrated at the Kelvin Hall Show in 1975. The Ailsa buses soon proved to be useful additions to the fleet based at Larkfield Garage but there were problems to be overcome. When drivers' protection screens were fitted to AV4-18, it was found that the cab, access to which was by means of the offside hinged door, became stuffy. The engine was beside the driver, it will be recalled. Additional signalling windows were fitted to provide extra air and AV16 had an additional air intake grille fitted above the driver's offside window. No platform hand rail poles had been provided due to the complicated three-leaf folding door getting in the way. Complaints were numerous and, when AV9 was de-roofed in 1976, it emerged from the Bus Works with a centre pole. These were subsequently fitted on all the AV-class vehicles.

Due to the box-like rigid structure of the Ailsa chassis and the front engine design and layout, their panoramic-windowed bodies did not suffer the flexing and twisting on the contemporary Atlantean equivalents and have so far escaped the problems with Atlanteans LA751-1350 (q.v.)

No more Ailsas were purchased until 1981 when ten B55 Mk III chassis were delivered with W. Alexander R-type bodies. These entered service in June, five with Voith (A1-5) and five with SCG auto-transmission (A6-10). The last one was repainted in West Midlands PTE livery and operated in that fleet as No. 7053 but retained its own fleet plates! Before returning to Glasgow, it also visited Merseyside and South Yorkshire. A1 travelled to Dublin to appear at the UITP conference in 1981.

The R-type bodies with aluminium frames introduced a new interior design with black vinyl seats, black fibreglass staircases, wood effect formica and patterned ceilings. Although A1-10 had grey seat frames, all the others were bronze. The fitting of the rear registration plates between the decks on A1-10 precluded the placement of external adverts at this position so future deliveries had the registration plates fitted below the lower deck windows. September 1981 saw a further 30 B55s with SCG transmission, A11-40. At the Kelvin Hall in November, A40 sported 'Strathclyde' fleetnames. The following year, A41-81 were built with sliding—rather than hinged—doors to the driver's cab and full length hopper vents. The larger destination screen layout was fitted to A41 upwards. Most unusually for Glasgow, three buses were renumbered not long after delivery. KGG 120Y (A60 new) was fitted with SCG transmission and, in order to group the two types of gearbox together, A60 was renumbered A81. SCG buses were A62-81. KGG 125Y (A65 old, A61 new) had also air suspension—the first B55 chassis so equipped; it was in fact an extra bus from that order. A60 was in service before being renumbered A81 while A64 was shown at an engineering exhibition at the Kelvin Hall in 1982.

Volvo had produced an underfloor-engined coach chassis known as B10M and the PTE purchased one (the prototype) for evaluation as an 86-seat double-decker with Marshall body. At 31ft. 9in.long and 14ft. 7in. high, AH1 (Ailsa Horizontal (engined)) was quite definitely the largest capacity bus in the fleet and was the fourth underfloor-engined double-decker to operate in the UK. In June 1982, A82-92 arrived, and by October, up to A116 had been delivered. Voith Transmission was specified for these buses, the last eight having air suspension. Just before this batch appeared, a B55 Mk III chassis with a Marshall 51-seat single-deck body was purchased from Volvo. Built to the order of Tayside Transport the bus was non-standard, with a blue and white interior. Once the PTE livery had been applied, and the bus numbered AS1, this extra long vehicle entered service with 'Strathclyde' above the doorway ... there was no room on the offside for the fleetname!

As a result of the experience gained in operating AH1, Ailsa-Volvo introduced a revised chassis to be known as 'Citybus'. Five were ordered with W. Alexander bodies incorporating electric wheelchair lifts at the front door, following the successful use of such equipment on the single-deck Metroliners. While 47 passengers could be seated on top, the bottom deck had only room for 27, using a combination of tip-up and conventional seating. AH2-6 entered service in 1984 and AH4 was the last PTE bus to be shown at the Kelvin Hall in November 1983. Once the batch was ready, the buses were sent to Maryhill Garage in time for its closure and then to Possilpark.

Preceding the arrival of fifteen more B55s came two 'white elephants' in the form of ex-demonstrators with Marshall bodies. Fitted with plush-looking brown upholstery and exposed lighting tubes, they were significantly 'different'. Standard PTE destination equipment was fitted and when they entered service A117 and 118 soon drew complaints of poor visibility from the rather low driving position. The cab floors had subsequently to be raised. A117/8 had Voith gearboxes and leaf springs.

Arriving a year late, the last batch of Ailsa B55s (A119-133) had SCG transmission. Repositioning of the interior heating equipment allowed the offside front seat nearest the stairwell to face forward unlike the previous buses, which had this seat facing backwards. As with all B55 double-deckers, the front axle weight limit does not permit any seats at the extreme front of the upper saloon.

Leyland

If the front-engined double-deck bus was to be the answer to operators' prayers, British Leyland engineers thought rather differently in producing a new generation single-deck bus. After the formation of the National Bus Company, a joint venture was started with Leyland which would provide the NBC and others with a vehicle designed for all types of operation but having a very strictly standardised basic specification. The engine was placed at the rear and operators could chose various lengths and door options. The Leyland National, while quickly 'accepted' by NBC and other fleets, was slow in arriving north of the border. Indeed, the largest fleet was to be found in Aberdeen (20), with others in independent companies. While these Nationals were claimed to be the 'ultimate' bus, there were many critics.

At the 1973 Kelvin Hall Show an example fitted with coach seats, (KRM 148M) and marketed as a 'Suburban Express' National was on display. Glasgow operated it on service 39 in June 1974—a luxury coach running to Pollok, or so the passengers thought! With limited experience of such buses, it was indeed a surprise when the PTE ordered twenty in 1978. The Leyland Nationals were being built at the purpose-built factory at Workington designed to cope with greater numbers than were actually required. Quick delivery was therefore possible and within a few weeks in February-March 1979, all 20 had been delivered in all-over white. The Leyland specification was inspired by Henry Ford: any colour

The three Marshall-bodied double deckers in the fleet bear a family resemblance. A118, one of the pair based on Volvo Ailsa B55 Mark III chassis, loads up for Castlemilk at St. Enoch Square. The driver seems to be half way between the top and bottom decks.

could be specified, as long as it was NBC red, green or white! After the PTE had added a green and yellow skirt, 'GG' symbols and fleet number plates, LN1-4 were officially handed over at a ceremony at Kelvingrove Park on 28th February. They were used on the Hillpark route alongside the Seddon midibuses, a short-lived Centre-circle (77 and 88) and a new service to Rutherglen (36). Two, LN19 and 20, were shipped to Islay off the Scottish West Coast to maintain services formerly operated by Maroner, which had ceased trading.

In the late 'seventies, British Leyland was planning a replacement chassis for the Atlantean, and out of the design for the integral rear-engined Titan bus (see *Chapter 13*) came a separate chassis, known at first as the 'B45', which could be bodied by builders other than Leyland. The name Olympian was given to it in 1980. One of the first examples to appear was the PTE's LO1. This bus was on show at the National Exhibition Centre in 1980 in a revised PTE livery of yellow, green and black. It also carried the first example of W. Alexander's R-type body, coupled with a 'transitional' interior finish from the last batch of Atlanteans. There were moquette seats, both saloons had white ceilings with black window surrounds and an electric destination display was fitted. Used as a demonstrator, LO1, with its Hydracyclic gearbox was not delivered or purchased until April 1981. As the prototype and first production Olympians were built at the Bristol Commercial Vehicles factory at Bristol, LO1 was licensed as a Bristol. It entered service from Maryhill Garage in the summer. Some 45 Olympians followed

with Charles Roe bodies—the first ever in the fleet—(LO2-11), Eastern Coach Works (LO12-16, 22-46) and W. Alexander (LO17-21). The ECW buses were of a lowheight design, the first since the war.

MCW

As was seen earlier, the eighteen Ailsa-Volvo buses had heralded the start of new thinking in the psv industry. However, the Metropolitans had been less fortunate and, in 1978, an all-British double-decker, the Metrobus Mk I was introduced by MCW, being powered by Gardner or Rolls Royce engines. One of the prototypes registration No. TOJ 592S (a two-door example) was used on service 2 (Rutherglen-Knightswood) for two days in April 1978. The livery on this bus was the forerunner of the 1980 PTE livery stage III. An additional white band beneath the lower deck windows was not adopted. As one would have expected by then, with the Glaswegians' inherent mistrust—and misuse—of two-door vehicles, the centre exit was not used. Its appearance in Glasgow coincided with a procession of vehicles and an Open Day at Larkfield Bus Works. Five production Metrobuses were ordered for evaluation and 'M43' was handed over at Buchanan Bus Station on 17th April 1979. It had been intended to number these buses M41-45, following on from the Metropolitans, and although fleet plates and internal transfers were applied, the bus entered service with MB3 outside and M43 inside (for a short time). Having MCW bodies, MB1-5 were fairly similar to the Metropolitans, with air suspension and Voith transmission.

Internally, they had moquette seats and a non-standard colour scheme of mustard and white. Based initially at Parkhead Garage, their hydraulically-operated braking system was later altered to conform with subsequent deliveries.

In 1982 came fifteen Metrobuses with W. Alexander R-type bodies with the revised destination layout. R-type windscreens differed according to the make—Metrobuses and Olympians utilized flat glazing, as opposed to the curvaceous Ailsas. The following year saw a further 25, this time with MCW bodies, the last two having Cummins engines. About a year after it entered service, MB35 was used in the Works for experimental trials with interior coach trim. Following this up, MB22 was refurbished internally with coach seating, carpeting, full interior software trim and luggage pen downstairs, which rather reduced the seating capacity. After removing the side number box, the bus was painted in a double-deck version of the Metroliner style. Further conversions involved MB23-26, but with a less luxurious finish, no luggage rack and side number box intact. This increased the seating capacity downstairs from 23 to 29. MB35 was altered subsequently to incorporate an electric lift at the front step in keeping with the Citybuses, the two-piece glider doors being replaced by a four-leaf arrangement. Tip-up seats left enough room for wheelchairs, whilst allowing 23 passengers to sit down.

Seddons

Whilst strictly speaking the inclusion of these six little midibuses in this Chapter

C1, the Bristol coach, was diverted from the Leicestershire fleet of West's Coaches, and its livery was adopted by the PTE until 1984 for coaches and tour vehicles. The PTE names had yet to be added in this view.

may be considered slightly misplaced, the purchase of these buses was a new venture for the city and it is convenient to include them under the heading 'New Generation'.

There were areas of Glasgow where full-size psv buses could not penetrate due to width and length restrictions. Glasgow's Hillpark area was a good example with narrow winding roads serving the estate. Thoughts turned to smaller psvs known as 'midibuses'. Greater Manchester PTE operated several buses of this type and its No. 1735, a Seddon Pennine 4-236 with Pennine 19-seat body, was inspected in Glasgow in August 1977. It was agreed to purchase four of these buses and the first two, Nos. 1703 and 1705, were delivered on 16th March 1978. After having a new livery of white with a yellow and green skirt applied, S1 and 2 entered service on 24th April on the new service 97 from Shawlands Cross to Hillpark. Three days later, S3 and 4 (formerly GMT 1700 and 1707) were received, and between them, these little buses were a 'roaring' success. They were the first second-hand buses ever bought but, with their manual gearboxes, a special rota of drivers who were licenced to drive them was needed. To operate a new service (98), between Queen Street Railway Station and Glasgow Central Station, a further two Seddons were acquired. Numbers 1736 and 1735 became S5 and 6. However, automatic gearboxes were fitted to this duo.

Coaches

Up until 1976, very limited use had been made of Glasgow's buses for Private Hire work. In fact, due to the recurring driver shortage, it was actively discouraged! Panthers were used for internal hires and outings with varying degrees of success (and failure!). When the popular 'Glasgow 800' tours were introduced in 1975, it was realised that valuable work was being lost due to the lack of suitable

vehicles. In April 1977, the first proper coach was delivered in the form of a Bristol LHS6L with Plaxton Supreme 35-seat body. It was intended for the Leicestershire fleet of West, Great Glen and finished in their livery of white, ochre and brown. C1 (VDS 216R) with its manual gearbox, re-introduced this form of transmission (last seen on BS1 in 1953!) and was the first Bristol to be owned since 1924. Initially, it was used for recreational work within the Department. To supplement this coach and for use on public tours, two Leyland Leopards with Duple Dominant II Express 51-seat bodies were purchased. Numbered C5 and 6, they were delivered in May 1978, followed closely by the rebuilt Panthers mentioned in *Chapter 9*. In the next two years further Leopards were built with similar coachwork (C7-12).

To cater for disabled passengers, two Metroliner coaches were purchased in 1983. C13 and 14 had luxury coachwork with a completely interchangeable form of seating. Up to twelve wheelchairs could be carried and by using tip-up side-mounted seats, there was also room for 24 passengers. If full luxury specification was required, the internal seating could be removed and replaced by 49 coach seats. Electric lifts were fitted to aid the carriage of wheelchairs. Cummins engines, air suspension and either a Voith D854 gearbox (C13) or ZF 5HP500 gearbox (C14) were specified. As a back-up, Leopards C5 and 9 were altered to incorporate wheelchair lifts to the rear of the back axle.

The last full-size coaches purchased by the PTE were delivered in 1985. C15 was a Volvo B10M with Plaxton 53-seat body, while C16 was a Leyland Tiger TRCLXC/2RH-34 with W. Alexander 53-seat coachwork. One of the 1974 Volvo double-deckers (AV10) was rebuilt in the Works as a single-deck bus after accident damage. Plans to extend the chassis to the dimensions of AS1

were dropped and the 'new' saloon vehicle—now AS2—entered service in the coach livery with seating for 38 passengers in a very odd-looking body.

In the summer of 1986, two Volvo coaches were hired for private hire and excursion work—C347 GSD with Caetano Algarve H-SDH body and Van Hool Alizee bodied A641 UGD.

Microbuses

The PTE's fleet of 'M'-class vehicles had all been withdrawn by July 1982, yet by the summer of 1983, another 'M' species had materialised—complete opposites in every way. An experimental service was planned to penetrate areas where access by normal size buses would be difficult. The concept of a 'taxi' like network would be possible using small vehicles. The PTE decided to market these buses under the name 'Microbuses' although this name had been used to describe Volkswagen's rear-engined van in 1954. Nevertheless, four Bedford CF350 chassis with Dormobile bodies were placed in service between Cadder and Maryhill Shopping Centre: the same route, it may be recalled, which had led to the purchase of the Albion single-deckers in 1939. Further 1983 deliveries included Volkswagen LT vans, Renault Masters, Ford Transits and Dodges with a variety of bodybuilders, seating capacity and liveries. Two ex-Greater Manchester Bedford/Reeve Burgess vehicles (M20 and M21) were hired for some time and entered service in GMPTE livery. They were repainted later but, after only seven months in the fleet, were purchased and promptly sold.

Three small psv buses used by financially-supported operators in Strathclyde Region were numbered into the fleet in 1986. YKN 324X, used by McKinnon of Colonsay, became M26; A614 TGD, used by McNair of Girvan became M27 and a Dodge GO8 in use on Arran became M28. This last-

Argyle Street's pavements have been widened to cope with erratic shoppers and L01 which was the third of the B45 prototypes for the Leyland Olympian, threads its way along this busy road. It was one of five of the B45 version which appeared at the 1980 Motor Show, this one introducing Alexander's R-type body, but did not enter service until 1981. The electronic destination was caught in mid change when photographed. Later, when the overall advert for Drugs Abuse was terminated, standard destination equipment was fitted.

Having been hidden from the light for years, Stockwell Street has occasionally basked in strong sunshine since the demolition of the former G&SWR terminal and its bridges. The passengers on A11, one of ten Volvo Ailsa B55 Mark III buses with Alexander R-type bodywork, are making full use of the hopper vents on their bus. Later deliveries had full width versions.

When a special one-day conference on Sport-Aid for the Disabled was held at Bellahouston Park, the PTE operated several vehicles to this venue, including the two Metroliner coaches built in 1983 and having seating adapted for wheelchair use. Both have Cummins engines but the vehicle shown, C14, is the one with ZF automatic gearbox.

Modifications made to two of the Leopard coaches with Duple Dominant II Express bodywork were the addition of a ramp to gain wheelchair access behind the rear axle and the removal of some seats in that section. As with all PTE coaches, C5 carried no external fleet number. This short-lived service (154) with an escort was seldom busy — certainly no exception here.

mentioned vehicle aroused particular interest because of the demountable body which was supplied by Marshall. When not required, it could be replaced by an enclosed van body. It was thought that this arrangement would suit small rural communities where such vehicles could play a dual role in providing for the needs of the populace. B949 YHS was delivered to Glasgow in red/black livery. Before crossing to Arran, however, the coach livery was applied. This experimental idea was funded in part by Strathclyde Regional Council. In its two years of operation, the vehicle's freight potential has seldom been exploited.

By September 1986, further additions to the Microbus fleet included M29, a Mercedes/Reeve Burgess combination and M30-31, Mercedes with W. Alexander conversion bodies. M32, a Wright-bodied Dodge, was the last vehicle to be delivered to Strathclyde PTE.

As part of the change to a private company, due to take place before 26th October 1986, buses began to appear in July with 'STRATHCLYDE'S BUSES' fleet name and new legal lettering. The Headquarters was to be situated at Larkfield Garage. M29 was the first bus to be delivered with this new nomenclature. The PTE announced that there would be no change to the livery of the ex-PTE fleet. To make the organisation more efficient, a drastic cut in both the bus fleet and personnel was necessary. Two garages, Newlands and Gartcraig, were closed in August, and a reduction in the Bus Works' staff meant that greater space for parking operational buses at Larkfield Garage was found. The 'Commercial Network' as laid down by the Transport Act 1985 was about to become a reality. The story of the Glasgow Bus fleet beyond this point is outwith the scope of this publication. Time will tell if the City's public transport network survives yet another upheaval. One can only speculate as to the size, colours, services and management of 'Glasgow's Buses' in the future.

Ailsa-Volvo

Bodies: AV1-9, 11-18, A1-133 have W. Alexander 79-seat bodies. AS1 has a Marshall 50-seat (originally 51-seat) body.
Registrations: AV1-3: GGG 300-2N; AV4-18: MGE 179-193P; A1-10: TGG 377-386W; A11-40: CSU 219-248X; A41-59: KGG 101-119Y; A60: KGG 141Y; A61: KGG 125Y; A62-64: KGG 122-124Y; A65: KGG 121Y; A66-80: KGG 126-140Y; A81: KGG 120Y; A82-96: OGG 178-192Y; A97-105: A560-568 SGA; A106-116: A732-9/41-3 PSU; A117-8: A483-4 UYS; A119: B999 YUS; A120-133: B21-34 YYS. AH1 is ESU 378X. A600-604 TNS were allocated to AH2, 3, 5, 4 and 6. AS1 is NHS 782Y.
A78, 117, 118 have had passenger-operated change giving machines installed from time to time.

Leyland

Nationals LN1-20 were registered GGE 156-175T and seated 41 passengers. LO1 has a B45-TL11/1R chassis, is registered VGB 346W, and has 46/30 seats.
LO2-46 have ONTL11/1R chassis and have registration numbers:
LO2-16: CGG 825-839X; LO17-21: ESU 4-8X; LO22-41: KGG 142-161Y; LO42-46: A731-5 TGB.
Seating. LO2-11 have 46/31 seats; LO12-16, 22-46 have 47/31 seats and LO17-21 have 47/29 seats.

MCW

MB1-5 were registered GGA 750-754T; MB6-20: EUS 101-115X; MB21-30: KGG 162-171Y; MB31-35: MUS 309-313Y; MB36-45: A730-739 RNS. MB6-20 have W. Alexander 45/33 bodies while the rest have MCW bodies with 43/23 coach seats (M22), 43/29 coach seats (M23-6) or 46/31 bus seats (remainder). Chassis types: MB1-5: DR101/5; MB6-20: DR102/26; MB21-30: DR102/31; MB31-43: DR102/36; MB44-5: DR132/4.

Seddons

S1: XBN 976L; S2: XVU 335M; S3: YDB 453L; S4: XVU 337M; S5: GND 509N; S6: BNE 729N.
S1 and 3 had seating for 25 passengers, S2 for 21, S4 for 23, S5 for 19 and S6 for 18.

Coaches

Leyland Leopard coaches C5-12 have PSU3E/4R chassis and were registered BNS 234-5S (C5-6); JGE 27-30T (C7-10); OGD 659-660V (C11-12). C13 and 14 have Metroliner chassis type CR 126/3-4 with MCW 49-seat coachwork and are registered A740-1 RNS. Volvo B10M-56 C15 is registered B730 CHS and has Plaxton 53-seat coachwork and C16 a Leyland TRCLXC/2RH with Alexander 53-seat coach body is B200 DGG.
C5 was altered to carry 27 passengers with three wheelchairs, whilst C9 can carry 37 passengers plus one wheelchair.

Microbuses

Bedford. M1-4 (OGD 240-3Y) Dormobile body with 16 seats.
Volkswagen. M5-7 (ONS 531-3Y); M10/1/6 (A762-4 THS); M22 (B688 AGD); M23-5 (B380-2 AYS). M5-7 have LT28D chassis, rest are LT31D. All have Devon Conversions 12-seat bodies.
Renault. T35D chassis with SPTE 12-seat bodies. M8-9 (A725-6 RDS); M12 (A109 SHS); M13 (A112 SHS).
Dodge. S46 with Reeve Burgess 17-seater body; (M14/5: A495-6 TSU).
Ford Transit. Dormobile (M17) or Mellor (M18-9) bodies with 16 seats; M17 (A46 NKE) ex-demonstrator; M18-9 (A348-9 VDS).
Bedfords M20 and 21 were XRJ 9S and AJA 4T. (CFS models with 15-seat Reeve Burgess bodies, ex-Greater Manchester 1747/6).
Mercedes. 608D chassis with Reeve Burgess (M29) or W. Alexander (M30/1) bodies; M29-31 (C683/4 LGE and C124 LHS) M32 (D364 OSU) is a Dodge G08 with Wright 24-seat body. M26 (YKN 324X), used by McKinnon on the Isle of Colonsay was a Bedford CF with Dormobile 16-seat body. McNair's bus (M27: A614 TGD) was a Bedford VAS5 with Reeve Burgess 16-seat body which had some cargo space. Arran Coaches M28 (B949 YHS) was a Dodge G08 with Marshall 20-seat demountable bodywork.

First away from the lights at Broomielaw, LO2, the first of the Roe-bodied Leyland Olympian buses dating from late 1981, leads the field of cars, a Mark II Metrobus and an SBG ex-London Transport Fleetline, bound for the former GCT outpost of Kilbarchan. LO2 in the original yellow, green and black livery, has one of the only ten bodies ever supplied to the Glasgow fleet by the Leeds-based bodybuilder.

The Metrobus Mark II design had deeper windscreens than the Scottish-built equivalents, or the MCW Mark I deliveries. Behind MB30, one of 25 of the complete MCW package (chassis and body) dating from 1983, is one of the ex-South Yorkshire PTE articulated buses used by McGill of Barrhead.

Intense competition between manufacturers in the early 'thirties led makers to go to great lengths to ensure that demonstration buses seemed at home in the fleets to which they were sent. The Bristol Tramways & Carriage Co Ltd was still actively striving for business in the municipal market in 1932, when this G-type with the six-cylinder JW petrol engine was provided with a Glasgow-style Cowieson body and painted in appropriate colours.

Registered HY 6605 in August of that year, it was sent as a demonstrator to Glasgow, but attracted no orders. It returned to Bristol, entering service with BTCC's own fleet in May 1934, being rebodied twice and receiving a Gardner 5LW engine, remaining in service until 1957 — from 1950 it somewhat resembled a post-war standard K5G, having received a lowered PY2-type radiator as well as a new ECW body.

Chapter thirteen: 'Odd men out'

If the reader has stayed the course this far in the story of the Glasgow Bus, he will have realised the importance of the adage 'Try before you buy'. It has long been the custom for manufacturers to supply demonstration vehicles to operators, providing the opportunity to examine and in many cases operate them under local conditions.

Glasgow Corporation has had its fair share of such buses, many of which have already been mentioned, where relevant, in previous chapters. Others have not been so easily categorised and fall into the 'Odd Men Out' class.

Most demonstrators which appeared for perusal before the war have already been detailed. The late 'forties saw Britain's public transport at its peak and many and varied were the vehicles on

the market. One of the first double-deckers to visit Glasgow after the war was a Foden PVD6 with Scottish Aviation body (JGD 675). It was unlikely to have entered service but was observed in Ibrox Garage around 1950. While Foden was attempting to enter the psv market, this example was in actual fact a demonstrator for the bodybuilders. Although fitted with rear platform doors and a Foden full-width front, it was very similar in appearance to Glasgow's D61-65. The bus was acquired by Garelochhead Coach Services in 1951. Ironically, both chassis manufacturer and coachbuilder faded from the psv scene and emerged in later years in other ventures.

In the early 'fifties, the swing towards single-deck buses with underfloor

engines was gaining momentum and several demonstrators of this style visited the City. A Leyland Olympic (KOC 242) with MCW 40-seat body was used on the Knightswood-Rutherglen service (2). It will be realised that single-deckers had (and have not) played a major role in the bus fleet, nevertheless others were equally determined ... NLP 635 (AEC Monocoach) with Park Royal body was used in service in 1955; LJW 336, a GUY LF model with Saunders-Roe body, was also inspected. An interesting visitor during 1956 relates more to the 'Glasgow trolleybus' story. An export model Leyland Olympic — 36ft. long — was used to test clearances on the former tram service 12 route before the introduction of the ten extra long trolleybuses which required

Crossley Motors Ltd had gone a stage further in registering one of the first examples of its Condor double-deck model in Glasgow as GE7974 as well as having it painted in complete GCT livery, including lettering and the municipal crest. The body, however, was built by Brush to a variant of that bodybuilder's own style. It was operated by the Department in February 1930, but then went on to Aberdeen when it was not only purchased but further orders for Crossley buses were placed. At Glasgow, there was to be just one Crossley in the fleet, in 1947 as shown on page 32.

The trend towards lighter vehicles continued into the double-deck market, and several companies provided examples of 'thinned down' models. This 1953 Regent III in City of Oxford livery had the 7.7-litre engine, much as used in Glasgow's Regents of the late 'thirties, a synchromesh gearbox and bodywork by Park Royal which contributed much to the weight reduction. Registered 7194H, it ran in Glasgow on services 2 and 11.

In 1953, several chassis makers turned towards lighter designs. London Transport conducted trials on country and Green Line routes with three lightweight single deckers of AEC, Bristol and Leyland make. The prototype integral AEC-Park Royal Monocoach was registered NLP 635 in a series largely issued to RT-type double-deckers and subsequently visited several other operators as a demonstrator, still in Green Line colours. It was used in Glasgow on services 20 and 25. The remains of the tram overhead at the canal bridge at Kilbowie Road, Clydebank can be seen in this view.

special dispensation. This Olympic, as will be gathered, did not carry fare-paying passengers but did lead to the introduction of longer single-deckers throughout the UK.

In 1966, wearing a pseudo-Leeds City Transport livery of two-tone green, came LYY 827D, an AEC Swift with 48-seat Marshall body with dual entrance/exit. It was used on service 21 (Pollok-Midland Street), a favourite for demonstrators, and a year later, in 1967, a Bristol RELL6L (LAE 770E) with brown and cream ECW body followed in its 'tyre tracks'. These trials took place while the Department debated the use of single-deck omo against double-deck crew-operated buses. Just after the GCT/PTE take-over in 1973 came a Volvo B59-56 single-decker VEB 566L with Marshall Camair bodywork and it was operated from Newlands Garage on services 21 and 39.

Double-deckers also made their appearances. In June 1960, 7800 DA, a Guy Wulfrunian, was used on service 4 (Balornock-Drumoyne). This yellow and cream painted vehicle was of an advanced design—so advanced that it failed to make much of an impression on the traditionalists amongst the country's operators and was not the success Guy Motors had hoped for. The best known of Glasgow's visitors must be, without doubt, 747 EUS. Albion Motors had introduced its 'Lowlander' model in 1961, largely in response to SBG demand for a low-floor equivalent to the PD3, and this bus, an LR1 example with semi-automatic gearbox, was displayed inside the Kelvin Hall in 1960. The W. Alexander body fitted seated 72 passengers and externally (and internally) the finish was to GCT specification. Obviously Albion (really Leyland!) had hopes of sales, but someone must have known that 229 forward-entrance buses were on order and it was highly unlikely that a third chassis type would be wanted. At any rate, 747 EUS entered service from

Newlands Garage in March 1962 in the last GCT livery. No fleet number was carried (should it have been B139?) and technically the bus was 'on hire' for nearly a year. It departed eastwards to Edinburgh for further demonstration work and eventually found itself in the Ribble Motor Services, Preston, fleet. The fact that GCT had embarked on the Leyland Atlantean programme did not help matters, and no orders were placed for Lowlanders, although they were popular for a time in the Scottish Bus Group fleets.

Once the Atlantean fleet had been established, there were those who maintained that city fleets should comprise of separate entrance and exit vehicles. Before GCT started the process of taking delivery of 286 such buses (then converting them to single doorway!), KTD 551C, a Park Royal-bodied Atlantean, was used on service 61 (Tollcross-Maryhill) in January 1966. This was one of the busiest services and a good chance to evaluate a separate entrance/exit vehicle before too many were purchased, although it was three years before the first batch appeared ... and a further four before they stopped!

In the mid-seventies the earlier trend towards single-deck buses like the Leyland National and AEC Swift had been reversed. British Leyland had spent many years and vast amounts of money in searching for a double-deck bus to replace the ageing Atlantean and Fleetline. Their answer was the B15 project which, with Park Royal and London Transport, would see operators into the 'eighties with a vehicle which bristled with passenger comforts and reliability (hopefully). On a dismal day in December 1975, one of several prototypes paid a visit to Larkfield Bus Works and made several trips for PTE staff. NHG 732P was a two-door example in London Transport red. Production started in 1978 (christened 'Titan') but, plagued with difficulties including proposed moves to other

factories, the output of Titans was very slow. GGPTE ordered five buses and at the 1977 Kelvin Hall Show, one was displayed in PTE livery with a single doorway and seats for 73 passengers. Provincial and, especially, Scottish operators were concerned that only Park Royal bodywork could be fitted (thus giving no work to local concerns) and favoured a less complex design. Production delays, coupled with the closure of the Park Royal factory in 1980, meant that only a handful of buses was purchased outside London. Not long after production of the Titan moved to the National plant at Workington, London Transport announced it would have no further Titans after 1984. In response to demand, British Leyland had already announced that a conventional chassis (rather than an integral vehicle) would be produced (initially 'B45', then 'Olympian'). This proved more popular, and in due course L01 made its appearance (*Chapter 12*).

Most recent demonstrators have been: MUT 206W, a Dennis Dominator from Leicester City Transport (206) and operated on service 57 (Darnley-Ruchill) in December 1980-January 1981; Scania/East Lancs (MUT 265W), double-decker, used for several months at Maryhill Garage in 1981, and several midi buses in a search for a suitable replacement for the Seddons. London Transport Bristol LH6L (BL 22: KJD 422P) was used in 1981; a Leyland Cub (YBK 129V) with Wadham Stringer body in 1980; PKR 399W (a Dodge 50) with Rootes 25-seat body (1981) and a further Cub (OWG 257X) with Reeve-Burgess 33-seat body in 1983. A less successful visitor has been the Dodge 566C battery-electric 19-seater (TDB 202X) which was used on inter-station service 98 on two separate visits, both ending in a prompt return to the manufacturer. None of the foregoing has proved itself to be capable of withstanding the rigours of Glasgow's midi bus routes.

Larkfield Bus Garage first saw service buses in 1929, some seven years before this photograph was taken with Leyland TD4c 377 nearest the camera among the three Cowieson-bodied buses representing the latest additions to the fleet visible — one of the Albion Venturers is seen on the left.

How many of the Transport Committee would notice that Leyland Titan 237 had Gruss air springs (of the type familiar on the Gilford 1680T model) fitted as an experiment when they made their inspection of Knightswood Garage? Few would observe too, that 234 had lining applied to the green 'tween decks although removed from 237. A slip board along the sides provided extra route information.

Chapter fourteen: Servicing the fleet

As the newly-introduced bus fleet was purely an experimental exercise by the Tramways Department, temporary accommodation was necessary. The City's nearest tram depot (Parkhead) had been opened two years previously and an area was adapted to house the initial fleet of fourteen vehicles. Fortuitously, the location suited the first service, being only minutes from the Glasgow Green terminus. Use was made of the Corporation Central Garage in the city centre at West Graham Street, where buses were stabled overnight once the shuttle services to tram termini were started. In 1927 these shuttle services had been extended to the city centre and new premises were sought. Contracts worth over £30,000 were placed in 1928 with firms to enable the building of a custom-built garage at Eglinton Toll, just over a mile south of Glasgow Cross. This would provide accommodation for about 100 buses, but in the meantime space was found at Newlands Depot. The new garage,

called Larkfield, was formally opened by Baillie Burt (the then Transport Convener) in May 1929 and the fleet was re-allocated. Further services developed and use was made of a building at Finnieston, rented from 'Carlaw's Cars'. An extension to Larkfield was opened by Herbert Morrison, Minister of Transport on 19th January 1931, giving this garage space to allow learner drivers to acquire skills on the skid pan and other manoeuvres.

The need for further premises in the west end of Glasgow was obvious and, after visiting various European cities, transport officials returned with great admiration for Berlin's Municipal Garage. Plans were quickly drawn up and a building erected on ground purchased from the proprietors of the Jordanhill Estate. Work was completed by 23rd October 1932, the Lord Provost, Sir Thomas Kelly, performing the ceremony. Designed on the basis of the Berlin example, Knightswood Garage was claimed to be the largest

in Europe, with the capability of housing 260 buses. The garage employed an early form of electric night storage heater designed to take up surplus power generated from Pinkston Power Station, when all it served were night and early morning tramway services. This was stored and released during the day. The need for Finnieston and Newlands garages ceased, but much later the latter saw further motorbus operation.

On acquiring the former trams and depots of Paisley District Tramways Company on 1st August 1923, Elderslie became a far flung outpost in rural (at that time) Renfrewshire. Forty-nine of the ex-Paisley trams would have proved too tall had standard GCT top covers been added, and therefore remained open-top to negotiate the low railway bridges in Barrhead and Elderslie. On 1st May 1932, these open-toppers, the last examples in passenger service, were replaced by low height Leyland Titans. Service 12/12A, Paisley Cross—Johnstone or

Kilbarchan was possibly the only local bus route replacing trams which actually paid heed to Leyland's famous TD1 advert 'Bury your tram with a Titan'. Further tram/bus conversion occurred when the TD1 had been superseded by later models. Elderslie remained the most independent and smallest of GCT's garages, gaining an additional bus route in 1933 (service 17) when the Abbotsinch tram service was abandoned.

By 1933, garages at Parkhead, Larkfield, Knightswood and Elderslie housed a fleet of over 331 buses. Eight years later it had grown to 593, only outnumbered (in municipal terms) by Birmingham City (1016 buses) and Manchester Corporation (730 buses), although Glasgow had by far the largest tram fleet outside London. While the peripheral garages carried out routine maintenance, the buses were required to visit Larkfield for their 'dock overhaul'. Further extensions to the Works were completed in 1941 and the Bus Works became separate from Larkfield 'running' garage. The driving schools situated at Knightswood and Larkfield made use of bus '2' until 1939, although it has always been the practice to augment the permanent 'learner' buses with 'reserved' passenger vehicles. Several others from the initial batch were converted into service lorries, a practice which continued well into the 'seventies.

In 1943, ground was purchased from the Housing Department and an open-air garage (Ibrox) with limited pit and office areas was built. Several services were transferred from Larkfield and as new routes opened up, were allocated to the most convenient garage. A feature of Ibrox was the 'central heating' system whereby rows of pipes were connected to the vehicles' radiators. Hot water, therefore, effectively provided a warmer start up and kept the vehicle interiors tolerable during the winter mornings. This 'Radrite' system was also used at Parkhead and probably other garages and entailed a special connector to be fitted at the base of the radiator. With

the advent of rear-engined buses (and reliable anti-freeze!) the system fell out of use in the early 'sixties.

E. R. L. Fitzpayne became General Manager in 1943 and was to become the longest holder of this post in GCT's history. Some of his lesser known ideas stemmed from his days as Chief Engineer. He believed strongly in frequent oil changes (for the buses!) and it was ensured that each garage was properly equipped to carry out this procedure. The used oil was sucked out, taken to the main Works, cleaned and returned for further use. Again, special connection points were fitted to the engines (a bespoke item) and eased the fitter's task. It now seems highly unlikely that the process was carried out as frequently as the General Manager laid down—some engineers even today claim that it is dubious that a *weekly* oil change has any effect on bus engines. Most engineers, in reality, tried to use as much fresh oil as possible, rather than the recycled variety. The rear-engined buses of the post-1962 era again put paid to this routine.

In 1951, a report from GCT's Automobile Engineer was submitted to Mr Fitzpayne, who had asked for a report into the maintenance, operation and storage of the motorbus and trolleybus fleets. The underlying concern undoubtedly was the cramped condition in the various garages. The following figures amply illustrate his anxiety:- Elderslie 19; Ibrox 80; Knightswood 209; Larkfield 211; Parkhead 110; giving a total of 629. Larkfield had housed the trolleybuses from their introduction and 44 vehicles were installed in a purpose-built depot at Hampden in December 1950. This relieved the situation at Larkfield to a certain extent. Working conditions for the night shift staff were very unsatisfactory, with every available square foot of space used for bus parking. Only two garages at this time had mechanical washes: Ibrox and Knightswood—the remainder had to be content with mops and buckets! The obvious answer was new

premises. A new garage situated in the north-east of Glasgow was mooted but it was ten years before Gartcraig was functional. A short term solution seemed to rest in the conversion of tram depots, which would become vacant as the replacement programme got under way. Langside Depot ceased operating trams in September 1956 and by 17th November 1957, it was ready to receive motorbuses for services 4A, 5, 14, 29 and part of the 37. As will be noted in the Appendix IV, Langside had been used to store withdrawn buses in 1954. The interior layout of this building was such as to prevent the operation of Atlantean buses until much later than other garages. Two years before the tram services in Paisley were withdrawn Elderslie bus routes 12 and 41 were handed over to Western SMT in February 1955, although the 'garage', which had undertaken tramcar scrapping, remained in operation until May 1957 for trams. Possilpark Depot received motorbuses, some fifteen months before ceasing use as a tram depot in 1959. Although most were ex-tram services, Possilpark did take over Knightswood duties on the 8, 28 and 47 bus routes. The 'antipodal' garage for Possilpark is Newlands, scene of the early bus operation. A fleet of newly-built Daimler CVG6 buses was placed there for the replacement of tram service 8 on 15th March 1959. In June, the Rouken Glen 'circle' was fully diesel-operated when tram service 25 was changed to bus 45. Four months later Larkfield lost services 21, 32, 39 and 40 to Newlands which also gained the new 57, to replace tram service 14.

The garage which had been referred to earlier in the 1951 report was nearing completion and Gartcraig began operating in June 1961, relieving Parkhead of services 35, 46 and 51, followed by service 10 and single-deck service 30 in October. 1962 saw four further additions to Gartcraig's allocation, all existing services. Trams ceased operation in September 1962 and the Department still required space for the expanding bus fleet. It

No doubt the real reason for the photograph was to illustrate the chassis ramps newly installed at Ibrox Garage in 1951, but of more interest are the vehicles beyond. From left to right are, 706 and 712, AEC Regals of 1940; tow wagon TD1, Titan bus 99 of 1928; 658 — Regent/Weymann of 1939; a Roberts-bodied Albion, and, to the right, 621, from the last batch of Cowieson-bodied Venturers built in 1938.

At 12.30 am on March 22 1950 Knightswood Garage had lined up these vehicles for the following day's duties. Individually identifiable are Guy Arab/Pickering 58, Alexander rebodied TD4 L18, TD5/Cowieson 481, Guy/NCME 67, Regent III/Met Cammell A7, CWD6/Brush 157 (the Copenhagen Daimler), TD5/Cowieson 466 and TD5/Weymann 490.

was decided to use part of Govan trolleybus garage (known as 'Lorne School' to them and the trams!) for services 4, 15, 50, 52, 53 from Ibrox. The motorbuses outlived the trolleys there by only three years—the garage closed completely in 1969, all services going to Ibrox. The former tram depot, Maryhill, closed for railed vehicles in 1961, began operating a variety of routes from November 1962. It remained the smallest garage with a bus allocation rarely rising above 60. Partick, another tram depot, was converted to bus operation within two years of the trams' departure, and took many services from Knightswood. The only other 'custom-built' garage, post-war, opened at Bridgeton in 1965, relieving both Parkhead and Gartcraig of some buses and services.

The situation was static for three years after the PTE take-over in 1973. Rationalisation of the bus services and drastic economy measures paved the way for the closure of Bridgeton, followed by Partick in 1977. With the introduction of the new generation buses around 1979-81, Maryhill Garage was chosen as the 'Evaluation' Garage and its allocation of Atlanteans was dispersed to make way for the five Metrobuses MB1-5 (which had been at Parkhead) and new Ailsas, Olympians and Metrobuses. In 1984, this feature of Maryhill could not save it from closure and, along with Ibrox and Langside, it ceased operating in May. The 'evaluation' fleet was moved to Possil and Larkfield. By this time Knightswood had also received some R-type Ailsas—Gartcraig, Newlands and Parkhead remaining primarily Atlantean garages. The bus driving school at Knightswood was closed in December 1982, leaving sole responsibility for training drivers to Larkfield.

A glance at the service vehicle table (Appendix III) will reveal the extensive use of ex-psv vehicles for engineering purposes. Many of the 1939 AEC Regents which were rebodied in 1950 were in turn converted into tow wagons. Five AEC Matador trucks were acquired from the War Office in 1947, one being used by the Mains Department, while the remainder were used for heavy duty towing—initially in green, cream and orange, but later, in the usual maroon service fleet colours. By 1973, these venerable machines had been rebuilt with new cabins and AEC Regent V-fronts, and repainted into Verona green and white livery. In 1970, the Corporation had converted twelve ex-PD2/24 buses into lorries and painted them dark green and white. In 1975 a further example was converted and these were repainted Verona green.

In 1976, a Leyland Hippo Wreckmaster was acquired. This six-wheeled vehicle with 6-speed gearbox and power-assisted clutch was originally exported to Canada in 1969. When it was found not to conform with Canadian regulations, it was returned to Britain and subsequently found its way to Glasgow. It is fitted with a Leyland O.680 engine. To replace the Leyland PD2/24s, four ex-psv Leyland Leopards were acquired in 1982—three ex-Yorkshire Traction buses and one ex-North Western. These were rebuilt at Larkfield and emerged in gold cup yellow livery and the other service fleet vehicles were repainted also. A second-hand Dodge with lifting gear and two Bedford lorries have also been acquired.

There have been numerous other vehicles used by GCT throughout the years in the service fleet including many 'commercial' vans, gully emptiers, tippers and trucks, which are too numerous to mention in detail. However, a few of the more unique vehicles are worthy of note. GG 4333 was a Ford tractor, purchased 1931-2 for use inside the Bus Works (Larkfield). This was replaced in 1957 by a Ferguson tractor FYS 71. BCJ 633 was an Austin tower wagon, used by the Mains Department, Dalhousie Street. EGD 13 purchased also in 1939 was a mobile Miller crane, used by the Haulage Department. The smallest candidate must surely have been a 'road' roller (CGA 128)—purchased in 1938 and used at one time on the bowling greens at GCT's recreation ground, which was situated near Parkhead Garage.

The first Atlantean in the fleet, LA1, was receiving attention when caught by the camera at Larkfield Bus works. Note the position of the rear flashers when new. One bus (a Leyland PD2/24) is in original livery surrounded by re-painted W. Alexander or Weymann bodies on Daimler, Leyland or AEC chassis. A Gardner 6LW engine is due to be fitted and appears to have the Regent III style rear mounting behind the fluid flywheel, indicating that it is for one of the Regent V models so powered.

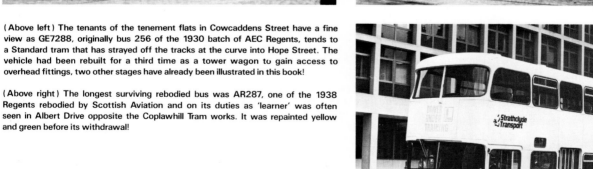

(Above left) The tenants of the tenement flats in Cowcaddens Street have a fine view as GE7288, originally bus 256 of the 1930 batch of AEC Regents, tends to a Standard tram that has strayed off the tracks at the curve into Hope Street. The vehicle had been rebuilt for a third time as a tower wagon to gain access to overhead fittings, two other stages have already been illustrated in this book!

(Above right) The longest surviving rebodied bus was AR287, one of the 1938 Regents rebodied by Scottish Aviation and on its duties as 'learner' was often seen in Albert Drive opposite the Coplawhill Tram works. It was repainted yellow and green before its withdrawal!

(Right) All-over white identified the PTE trainers and Atlantean LA697 shows off the modifications carried out for this work. The middle door — ignored by Glaswegians — has found a use at last. Access to the top deck is generally sealed off, despite the presence of seats, etc.

The 1928 order for 100 Leyland Titan double-deckers, following on almost immediately from an initial fifteen, was a break-through both for Glasgow and Leyland — although the TD1 model was an immediate success, this was easily the largest order placed in the early days of the model as well as making Glasgow a major double-deck bus operator despite the continued dominance of the tram. The use of cadmium yellow coupled with early photochromatic film has resulted in 109's lower panels appearing much darker. It sits amongst new Corporation houses attracting tenants and customers.

Chapter fifteen: The liveries of Glasgow's buses

During their entire life-span, Glasgow's famous tramcars were painted in a highly distinctive livery. Until the last years when the idea was phased out, the upper sides carried differentiating service colour bands. When married to transatlantic-inspired cadmium yellow lower panels, ornately lined-out, the effect was to brighten up the city streets which had yet to receive the skilled attention of the stone cleaning brigade.

The first Corporation buses appearing in 1924 were, of course, single-deckers and the painting style resembled the then recently-introduced single-decker trams for the Clydebank-Duntocher service. The question of service colours did not arise.

In 1928, however, there descended on Glasgow the first of the Leyland Titan TD1 lowbridge double-deckers. The use of service colours was just beginning to cause rostering problems on the trams. Should the new buses have their own house colour? If so, what should it be?

Obviously it had to be selected to avoid confusion with the red, green, blue, yellow or white trams which filled the main streets like some multi-coloured conveyor belt. In specifying the Leyland (or equivalent) bodywork with standard single aperture destination screens, there was no provision for displaying a service number. However, service numbers were employed eventually, once services expanded via stencils mounted behind the upper-deck front windows and this enabled a neutral colour to be selected for the upper-deck sides. This was most probably chosen on aesthetic (if not religious!) grounds and a most pleasant blend of green, cream and cadmium yellow was adopted from then on, lined-out in restrained fashion with white, black, green or orange. At the time, green was the second most numerous service colour on the trams but while this resembled the Verona green later used on PTE buses, the original bus green had more yellow pigment. To avoid

When 188's original Cowieson body was destroyed in an accident in 1931, it was re-bodied, uniquely, by tramcar and railway wagon builder Hurst, Nelson & Company of Motherwell. Two major differences from the specification of the first body are the unusual narrow front upper-deck emergency window complete with ladder and the cream-painted roof area.

GCT paid scant attention to wartime economies as far as painting vehicles was concerned. Regent 573 (wrongly numbered '753' above the filler cap) had received a larger area of green than normal, yet grey-wall tyres, varnish and wheel discs give no air of austerity. The 'streamlined' livery on the next bus has almost surrendered to the painter's brush.

The orange, green and cream livery as applied to one of the thirty Leyland Worldmasters fitted with GCT dual-doorway bodies on Weymann-built frames at Coplawhill from 1956. LS26 is seen at Clarkston terminus.

(Below) The all-metal W. Alexander bodies of 1957 lacked beading of any kind, yet the black lining was faithfully applied, and successfully separated the three colours. Black gloss wings reflect the Daimler motif on D135 which, unlike most of the batch, had hopper-type vents fitted downstairs. L49 also had these.

(Above) 1955-built Weymann-bodied Daimler CVG6 D95 arrived with most of its bodywork unpainted, but fortunately received the attentions of the paintshop after two years in service.

confusion with paint supplies, this paint colour was known as 'bus green' and remained described as such 40 years after the tram equivalent ceased to be ordered.

The full colour specification for the pioneer single-deckers was:

Panels with coat of arms	: Metropolitan yellow
Panels above coat of arms	: Straw
Rear end lower panel	: Metropolitan yellow
Rear end narrow panel	: Straw
Narrow panel, driver's compartment	: Straw
Lower panel, driver's compartment	: Metropolitan yellow
Beading around the panels	: Black
Glasgow Corporation letters	: Silver transfers 4¾in. Black relief ¼in.
Window posts	: Straw yellow, lined black
Roof	: Light grey
Wings	: Black with yellow line ½in. broad, 2in. from edge
Chassis, springs and undershield	: Crimson lake
Petrol tank	: Black
Wheels	: Crimson lake ¼in. broad yellow line — 2 on hub, one on rim
Steps	: Grey treads, black risers
Bonnet — fixed top	: Straw
Lifting side of bonnet	: Metropolitan yellow
Door handles	: Metropolitan yellow
Door rails and strikers	: Straw
Window frame in weather screen	: Metropolitan yellow
Framing of weather screen	: Straw
Panels of weather screen	: Metropolitan yellow

Another specification called for a white roof with outside ventilators in varnished mahogany.

The 'Straw yellow' was in fact a fairly deep cream, varnished and 'Metropolitan yellow' was cadmium yellow. This can still be seen today at the National Tramway Museum where it is carried by Newcastle tramcar No. 102. In Glasgow, from 1928 onwards, the cadmium yellow became progressively more orange. Latterly, paint suppliers' tins were endorsed 'Glasgow Corporation Transport — Orange'.

The 1928 deliveries lost nothing of the colour but the lining-out became much more modern even for the time. Any varnished wood disappeared from the exterior. Roofs became dark grey and while the lower saloon windows retained the cream colour, albeit minus black lining, those for the upper deck were 'bus green' unlined. Main colours were separated by beading which was lined in black. The orange panels had a fine white line applied near the top. The narrow cream panel below the lower saloon windows featured two fine orange lines while the equivalent panels below the upper saloon windows had two fine green lines. Legal lettering was black and silver — actually aluminium — transfers were identical to those on contemporary trams. This livery survived almost intact, losing only the fine lining, until 1938, when the green bands were downswept at each end to provide a streamlined effect. If this sounds vaguely familiar, it should, as it strongly resembled the styling employed on the 'Coronation' luxury tramcars which were being placed in service at this time. Even the

art deco interiors of these trams was repeated in the buses and many fittings were of identical specification. As to which came first, the answer probably is that the 'Coronation' tram took its inspiration from earlier buses although the streamlined buses were imitations of the trams.

The first streamlined buses were those with local Cowieson bodywork numbered from 435 upwards. These incorporated beading applied to the uppersides taking the contour of the black lining between the green and cream. The beading was to remain a prominent feature on many buses until withdrawn although, like all the 'streamliners', the paint style was simplified on the occasion of the first repaint. Weymann's interpretation was similar to Cowieson's but rather more flamboyant and not quite so subtle. When buses numbered 636 upwards appeared the following year the livery was simplified with green taken right up to the upper-deck window ledges. The window posts and roof were then cream.

Came the 1939 war and all protruding edges such as mudguards, platform edges and grab rails were overpainted white to suit black-out conditions. Initially the prominent 'GLASGOW CORPORATION' lettering was retained above the lower-deck windows but this was removed around 1942-3 concurrent with its removal from the trams (in their case it was on the rocker panels). Not for Glasgow the dark brown or grey roofs; these became matt green to be less conspicuous from the air at night. A few survivors from the pre-375 deliveries had their dark grey roofs painted green. Only Nos. 264 and 238 — which long outlived

their contemporaries — lasted long enough to acquire the later cream roofs which were specified again around 1948-49. Thus wartime conditions did not have the drastic effects on the Glasgow fleet painting style or finish as could be noted on London's buses or Liverpool's trams. Nevertheless, one or two bizarre examples were noted, with green extending over the entire upper-deck, as shown on No. 573; and as on Cowieson-bodied TD4s 397 and 402, in green, cream and **green** — where the orange should have been. TD1s 220, 279 and AEC Regents 547, 614 and 746 were mostly green with little orange or cream included. At least one bus operated with Garner's of Bridge of Weir in their full livery of red, brown and cream, but with GCT legal lettering. It was scrapped in 1949, still in this livery.

When the war ended in 1945, the only immediate change to the fleet was the removal, as opportunities arose, of the white paint from wings, etc, and roofs became gloss green instead of matt. During the war GCT had outshopped all repainted buses with grey tyre walls and this policy continued for some years. Around 1948 it was decided to revert to cream for roofs but, as often happens, news did not always filter through to the various coachbuilders for new buses then being completed to reflect this change in policy. So it was that A71 and A72 appeared with green roofs extended down at the rear to window ledge level, but with the rear emergency doors in cream. A73 and A74 were similar, but the emergency doors were green also. From A75 onwards cream roofs were standard. Crossley painted the bodies for A21-70 green downswept to cover the entire rear dome areas. These were all painted cream by GCT before the first overhauls. B1-49 and B89-98 were delivered with green roofs, as was C1, but the batch A1-20 displayed some interesting variations. A1-8 had green roofs, with cream dash panels and bonnet tops. A9-14 also had green roofs but without the attractive cream paint on the dash and bonnet. A15-20 had cream roofs when new. DS43 was painted in quasi-trolleybus livery with the orange supplemented by green surmounted with an orange stripe and cream upperworks. Anticipating later policy, the mudguards were also painted in the main body colour, in this case, green.

Having stabilised by 1950, the next minor change occurred with the delivery of L49. Bodywork on this vehicle displayed much of the drive towards lighter weight evident in earlier deliveries to Edinburgh Corporation which had Weymann or W. Alexander bodies. There was less beading on the body sides and the opportunity was taken to eliminate the cream band below the lower saloon windows and extend the green down to the top edge of these windows. After a while, some older buses also had the lower cream band eliminated. The 1955 Weymann and W. Alexander-bodied Leylands and

AECs had a much shallower green area. More was to come, however. In an effort to utilise spray painting techniques, simplification was pursued. L175 appeared new with the entire upper deck green and the entire lower deck in what seemed to be an uncomfortably 'hot' orange. These contrasting colours were separated only by a thin black line. L269 also featured this scheme. L119 had this translated into green and pale yellow. Coplawhill turned out a few older buses in the green/orange style with 7in. separating cream band above the lower deck windows. A94, A121 and D7 come to mind. L124-128 were despatched for service (from Coplawhill) identical to L119, then from L129 onwards until completion of the batch at L148 introduced the 7in. cream band as standard. This was not carried round the front except later when LA1 first appeared with this style, and LA2 (new). The first deliveries from Falkirk with the new green, cream and yellow 'spray' colours were L274 and D243, and initial repaints were brush painted before the spray painting plant at Larkfield Works was commissioned. Following this, it became possible and economical to paint each bus every two years instead of every four. It should be stressed, however, that the new finish was not as durable in the first place.

Parkhead Garage became well known for turning out buses with partial repaints. Some retained the old top-deck style with yellow lower deck and wings. Others retained the old lower deck cream and orange but with green roof and upper-deck window posts. Ibrox Garage staunchly retained black wings until it was forced to succumb to conformity. The original green, cream and orange disappeared by early 1965.

Placing the green over the yellow made the buses look rather top heavy. It also placed the lighter colour in a position which was vulnerable to damage and dirt. In this context there was logic in Mr Fitzpayne's experiments in 1964 with reversed liveries. These looked more acceptable to many — particularly on vehicles with less body moulding and beading which latterly had not featured in simplified livery styling. Most types in the fleet were treated — including D19 for a brief spell — but complaints abounded as to confusion in the minds of the public. As

they say in Hollywood (or was it President Reagan?) 'You ain't seen nothin' yet!' Read on ...

It was at this time that LS31 appeared for one-man-operation, painted in the new reversed livery. On these long single-deckers (plus LS26 later) the reversed livery was retained (as a means of identifying omo buses) but within a short period other 'upside down' buses were repainted right way up. There were claims that the shades of green and yellow used for this experiment were different from standard, but the normal colours were used. The shades of green and yellow were in a state of flux from 1961-63 until they settled. This depended very much on whether W. Alexander or GCT built the bodies, whether they were varnished (as when placed in service new) or despatched from the major overhaul, and of course the paint manufacturer. After some year's use, the platform used to lower and raise vehicles in the spray booth became defective. Unfortunately, L377 happened to be on the platform at the time and when the platform fell into the pit, L377 went with it. This explained the presence of a distorted, newly-painted bus in the scrap lye — much earlier than its fellow PD3s. A final GCT alteration to the livery occurred when LA601 upwards were delivered, with Brunswick green wheels taking the place of maroon, breaking a link with the trams. These LAs had black bumpers fitted, and made use of much larger fleet numbers front and rear. Rear-entrance buses had the stair risers and platform areas previously maroon, also painted Brunswick green.

When Greater Glasgow Passenger Transport Executive was formed, it introduced its first new livery in July 1973. This was applied to double-deckers with white being used for the roof and top-deck window surrounds, gold cup yellow for the top deck 'decency' panels, white for the lower-deck window surrounds and Verona green below. Rear engine buses had the engine compartments painted green also and those without shrouds had the green extended up to the overhang of the top deck. No doubt to mask the effects of oil spillage, the rear bumpers were black. This livery on LA700 and 703 was introduced to the public on 6th July 1973 and it was as well that the 12th

was avoided due to the similarity between the new bus livery and the Irish Republic flag! Very early repaints had Verona green wheels (including L118 and L347) giving rise to comparison with Dinky buses. Thankfully these and future repaints reverted to Brunswick green. It was stated at the time that these colours would conform to British Standards and also retained a link with past liveries. With many various hues of the SBG vehicles in the City, care had to be taken with the PTE's choice. However, it is known that the first Director General, Mr R. Cox, had favoured a blue/white livery and several drawings survive of his many ideas. In retrospect, there was little chance of a radical change on this emotive issue.

The first new buses delivered in the PTE livery were LA717-750, but some earlier ones from the same batch were placed in service with the new style applied at the Bus Works. The fleet numbers in these early days were black metal plates with the numbers embossed in aluminium. They were very hard to read despite their being applied for the first time on the near and offsides in addition to the front and rear. LA751 introduced white or yellow reflective plates with black figures and although L752-798 reverted to the silver transfers, LA799 onwards standardised on LA751's specification which gradually spread to all Atlanteans from LA651 upwards, new deliveries from then on, and to a few selected earlier vehicles such as those used for display at the Omnibus Society's Presidential Weekend in Glasgow in 1974. Not all the ex-GCT vehicles operated received the first PTE livery depending on their anticipated life-span. The PTE logo was applied on the forward near and offside upper panels and this was applied to earlier buses not destined for a repaint.

The Panther single-deckers had their own style with yellow roofs, white window surrounds and verona green lower panels. The yellow was extended down to meet the green at the rear. Seddon single-deckers had yellow roofs also, but only the skirt panels were Verona green, along with the radiator panels — the rest being white. The Leyland Nationals introduced a third variation. This time the whole bus was white down to a green and yellow skirt. All the single-deckers had Brunswick

The final GCT livery is well illustrated elsewhere in this book, and remained until PTE influence took over. The 'Reversed' livery was received with hostility and two examples are shown. A219, one of the Weymann-bodied Regent III buses, retained black wings, and in all cases the maroon wheels remained. The change suited modern vehicles such as 1962 Atlantean LA24 better, perhaps, than their older consorts.

green wheels and hubs. The only variant to the first livery was seen on LA795 which featured a much deeper yellow applied between 1980 and 1982 to test the colour's durability.

Legal lettering was black: 'GGPTE, 48 ST. VINCENT STREET, GLASGOW G2 5TR' replacing the old 'GLASGOW CORPORATION TRANSPORT, W. MURRAY, GENERAL MANAGER'. The fleet name 'Trans-Clyde' (black, edged white) was applied below the GG logo from October 1979 but in 1980 the 'GG' transfers were gradually removed. LA717-1410, 1413-1425, AV1-18, M1-40 and MB1-5 were delivered in this first stage PTE livery. When LA1220 was converted to an open-topper, it received its own version with yellow body, green domes and skirt and white band above the lower-deck windows. This scheme lasted from 1978-84. The other open-top Atlantean LA957 went straight into the current tour livery on its conversion.

The second stage livery appeared ever so gradually and without warning—with the re-introduction of spray painting. The colours were the same as before but the yellow was extended to cover the top-deck window surrounds and roof. Green was extended to cover the lower-deck surrounds except the windscreen remained white. A 7in. white band divided the two colours above the lower-deck windows. Remember Mr Fitzpayne's upside-down buses? Black skirts were added along the sides and rears. This livery only applied to Ailsa-Volvos and Atlanteans up to LA1426—not all were touched by any means. New deliveries from W. Alexander then had the heating system air intake louvres located immediately behind the driving cabin window. W. Alexander's coachpainters painted this part white, commencing the Verona green on the panel further to the rear. As would be expected, at least one Atlantean, LA873, had the top deck painted all over yellow but the bottom half of the bus was not repainted.

The second stage livery appeared first in September 1980—the same month that a **third** stage livery also appeared! This was displayed on the first Olympian, LO1, at the Birmingham Motor Show. The shades of green and yellow were the same, but the yellow was extended to the top of the lower-deck windows, whose surrounds became matt black, which was also used for skirt panels. White was thus eliminated. LA1411 and 1412 were also placed in service new, with this style although the green was not upswept on the rear engine shrouds as later became standard. LA1439 onwards featured the matt black finish as did A1-91, MB6-35, LO2-41 and AH1. LO1, AH1 and A40 used the fleetname 'Strathclyde' when new although LO1 reverted to 'Trans-Clyde' before entering service. Legal lettering was changed to white to appear on the black skirt panels (usually!).

A fourth livery (or perhaps more correctly stage 3A!) appeared on the Seddon midi buses S2 and S5 for use on the inter-station service 98. These were turned out in the first version of Underground Orange with a white band below the side windows and with orange wheels. 'Rail-link' boards were attached below the side windows. LA1295 was very briefly painted in this style (not unlike Cardiff City Transport livery) with the white band above the lower-deck windows, but never entered service in this scheme. LA947 was also uniquely painted in the yellow, matt black and green format except that the yellow was pale primrose (thought by some to be undercoat) and the green a richer and less 'plastic' than the erstwhile standard Verona green. This was evidently to test the durability of different shades and the bus was scrapped in this condition.

Yet another livery emerged in November 1982. A darker, more durable orange had been introduced for underground trains, known as 'hot orange' (aptly) then 'Govan Orange' and eventually 'Strathclyde Red' (!)—Standard Paint No. SP 8128 for all modellers who may be reading this chapter. It first appeared above ground on National LN15, incorporating matt black skirt panels, wheels and window surrounds. It was intended primarily for inter-station work, to complement the Underground trains and therefore also applied to Atlantean conversion SA1 in April 1983 as well as subsequent rebuilds. A change of policy dictated that from April 1983, this striking livery should apply to all 'Rail Replacement' services, hence LA1447 was thus repainted for service 94 (Crookston Castle—City Centre). It was not long before this livery was adopted for all PTE buses, British Rail local network rolling stock and underground cars. Plans which might have resulted in all Strathclyde Regional Council financially supported operators also having this livery imposed have not materialised. PTE buses delivered in this 'Strathclyde Red' scheme were A91 upwards, LO42-46, MB36-45, AS1 (although strictly speaking a repaint immediately taken into stock) and Micro-buses—except M8, 9, 19-21. At first the fleetname was 'Strathclyde' and this appeared on LA776, 1359 and 1447. All later repaints then had the stylised Regional map logo applied to the left of 'Strathclyde Transport'. LA1249 appeared with the fleetname on the yellow and green livery in the summer of 1984. Microbus M19 was delivered in all-over white while M20-21 were in their former Greater Manchester colours. When LA975 was converted to become a mobile survey bus (complete with gas lighting and a loo!) it carried its own version of all-over yellow with green and black skirt. Late in 1984, the bus underwent further internal alteration and became an exhibition vehicle, painted in normal 'red' and black. When the former GCT Head Office at 46 Bath

Street was closed along with the Executive offices at 48 St. Vincent Street, the new legal address was quickly applied to the bus sides (and underground stock): 'CONSORT HOUSE, 12 WEST GEORGE STREET, GLASGOW, G2 1HN'.

When the first proper 'coach'—C1—was delivered, the small Bristol was painted white with ochre and brown stripes in a contemporary style. This was adopted for C2-12. LN17 was painted in a simplified style and used for private hire as well as stage carriage work. It was repainted in bus livery later in 1984. Metroliners C13 and 14 introduced a white livery with Strathclyde red and black stripes. Microbuses M8 and M9 also carried this style and it was adpted for the Metrobus coach conversions (MB22-26) together with the City Tour buses LA1401-2 as well as open-toppers LA957 and 1220. By early 1985 it was being progressively applied to the remaining Leopard coaches.

Incidentally, tour liveries have differed since the introduction of these services. In 1977 buses used sported silver (with blue band): 1978, white (with salmon stripes): 1979, white (with blue lettering): 1980-4, white, ochre and brown: 1985-6, white (with red and black stripes).

In 1984 it was therefore possible to see all the main livery stages at the same time! LA683 was in service in August in the first PTE livery—a late example but soon to succumb to the spray gun. The last green, white and yellow bus was believed to be LA803, still painted this way in January 1985 (albeit in the driving school fleet). Several buses were running minus black skirts—still in green, black and yellow eg A8, LA1133, 1334. In February there remained about 100 buses not in 'Strathclyde Red' and a start was made in removing their 'Trans-Clyde' fleetnames and substituting 'Strathclyde Transport'. Interestingly, just as Ibrox Garage retained black mudguards long after it was abandoned in the final GCT livery, Knightswood Garage had most of its allocation of green/yellow buses' wheels painted black, to match the 'red' buses. This did not prevent the inevitable mix of wheel colours when punctures arose. By September 1985, there were no serviceable buses in any of the green/white/yellow/black schemes.

In June 1986, in preparation for the deregulation of local bus services and the acquisition of the PTE bus fleet by a new public transport company, Strathclyde Buses Limited, the fleet began to lose the 'Strathclyde Transport' logo and a new 'Strathclyde's Buses' logo was applied to the upper-deck front side panels, and also below the lower-deck side windows, at the front of most makes of buses and the rear panels above the lower-deck window in the case of the Ailsa buses.

No one could ever say that Glasgow has been a dull place these last sixty years!

An Omnibus Society Presidential Weekend line-up at Larkfield in 1974 illustrates the verona green, yellow and white livery with 'GG' monogram introduced by the new Greater Glasgow PTE a year earlier. Left to right in this specially posed view are D217, the unique Daimler CVD650.30 of 1958, AEC Regent V A350 and Leyland PD3/2 L404, all with Alexander bodywork. D217 had been exhibited at the Scottish Show in November 1957 before delivery. It was the only front-engined 30ft. Daimler in the fleet and as such had a wider front grille moulding. It had power-assisted steering as well as basically the same 10.6-litre Daimler engine as D60 of 1951. It was also the only motorbus of this length in the fleet to have a rear entrance.

S2, one of the four Seddons purchased from Greater Manchester PTE, is seen on the new route for which they were intended at Hillpark. The vehicle is in the GGPTE's original livery, although the yellow roof was scarcely visible from ground level.

The first orange livery chosen for the new Underground cars was applied to Seddons whose duties involved operation of the Inter-station service 98 between Queen Street and Glasgow Central. S5 is in George Square behind LA467 in original PTE colours.

Much attention was given to solving the problems which occurred on the long-windowed Atlanteans. LA1330 was one example where the bottom deck window pans were rebuilt, although not always symmetrically, or to all bays. Like the livery, Trans-Clyde fleet names and OMO sign, this particular service 15 disappeared, victim of relentless attempts to achieve viability.

Stage 2 and 3 liveries side by side at Cadogan Street. LA1292 has the high cab arrangement with deep windows. The saucer shape on the roof is the radio aerial. LA1072 is behind.

Whilst the passengers on LA1381 one fine summer's morning in 1984 seem to have taken the advice on the exterior, it may be sometime before the same can be said for the majority of Glasgow's upper deck travellers. The bus is heading towards the City on the diverted Maryhill Road near St. George's Cross.

Back to the beginning... Small-capacity single-deckers were in vogue again by the 'eighties. M18 of 1984 is a Ford Transit 16-seater whose Mellor body gives unrestricted views from the rather cramped interior. The black fleet number and wheeltrims proved to be short-lived features.

In monochrome, there is little obvious change to the colour scheme once the last PTE livery was applied, save that 'Strathclyde Transport' fleetnames are applied. Surprisingly, the bottom deck windows have gained small vents while upstairs the bus still has its original larger versions. An Alexander peak-domed Ailsa gives a fine comparison of front and rear engine design alongside.

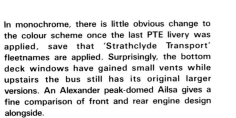

The elaborate colour scheme on the 'Citizens Theatre' bus shows up well in this view at George Square. The modified radiator grille is just discernable with its exposed filler cap. The small platform above the number box housed the radio aerial, but in this position was easily damaged by the bus wash, and soon had a protective sleeve added, misguidedly thought by some to be strengthening.

Appendix 1

Principal Post-War Orders

Date Announced	Chassis and Quantity	Proposed fleet numbers	Bodybuilder and Quantity	Proposed fleet numbers
November 1945	20 AEC 48 Albion CX19	A1-20 B1-48	44 MCCW 24 Roberts	A1-20, B25-48 B1-24
December 1946 %(1)	70 AEC 40 Albion CX37S 20 Daimler CVD6	A21-90 B49-88 D1-20	50 Crossley 40 Northern Coachbuilders 40 Roberts	A21-70 A71-90, D1-20 B49-88
December 1946 %(2)	75 AEC 25 Albion CX37S	A91-165 B89-113	75 MCCW 25 GCT	A91-165 B89-113
September 1947	43 Daimler CVD6	DS1-43	43 GCT 25 MCCW Frames	DS1-43 B89-113
May 1948	100 AEC 45 Daimler CVD6	A166-265 D21-65	100 Weymann 40 W. Alexander 5 Scottish Aviation	A166-265 D21-60 D61-65
1951	25 Albion CX37SW	B114-138	25 GCT	B114-138
April 1954	75 AEC 50 Daimler CVG6 25 Leyland PD2	A266-340 D67-116 L24-48	49 Weymann 26 Weymann 25 W. Alexander 49 W. Alexander 1 W. Alexander/MCW	D68-116 A315-340 L24-48 A266-314 D67
July 1955	200 Leyland PD2 50 Daimler CVG6	L49-248 D117-166	150 W. Alexander 50 W. Alexander 50 GCT	L49-98, 149-248 D117-166 L99-148
1957- 1958- 1959	1 Daimler CVD6-30 100 Daimler CVG6 100 Leyland PD2 140 Leyland PD3 89 AEC	D217 D167-216, D218-267 L249-348 L349-488 A341-429	101 W. Alexander 75 W. Alexander 50 GCT 115 W. Alexander 89 W. Alexander	D167-267 L249-323 L324-373 L374-488 A341-429

% Intended delivery: (1) 1947-48 (2) 1948-49.

Fleet No.	Advert	From	To
LA211	Carrick Store	1/73	4/74
LA230	Barclaycard	3/72	1/74
LA230	Barclaycard (revised)	1/74	1/76
LA231	Yellow Pages	3/72	4/73
LA284	BusyBee Store	2/74	1/78
LA290	Sony (Purple)	11/72	2/75
LA295	MacKays Store	12/72	4/75
LA300	Krazy House (Shop)	12/73	4/75
LA300	Krazy House (revised)	4/75	5/78
LA302	M & W Personnel	6/74	3/77
LA381	Transcard (yellow/white)	9/74	7/76
LA381	Transcard (blue)	7/76	5/79
LA391	Cameron & Campbell	12/74	1/76
LA404	Agnews Store	2/75	4/77
LA418	Glasgow 800 (Y)	4/75	10/75
LA425	Savoy Suite	7/75	10/76
LA429	G.G.H.B.	8/75	9/76
LA432	Glasgow 800 (W)	4/75	10/75
LA439	Citizens Theatre	10/75	12/76
LA442	Maryhill Carpets	10/75	2/77
LA476	D. Milne (Photographs)	2/76	6/76
LA480	Escariot (shop)	2/76	6/77
LA489	Blazes suite	3/76	8/78
LA636	Maryhill Carpets	11/78	9/81
LA692	Everton Mints	6/73	2/75
LA695	Castrol (broadside)	6/73	10/74
LA701	Balmore Bakeries	12/73	11/74
LA739	PTE recruiting	6/74	12/75
LA739	Transrail cards	12/75	2/77
LA768	Diamond Heavy beer	7/80	7/81
LA775	Phoenix Assurance	7/80	7/83
LA850	Carlsberg Lager	11/75	5/78
LA957	Open top (tours)	5/78	
LA995	Transcard (green)	12/77	3/80
LA1000	City Tour 1976 (Y)		10/76
LA1022	City Tour 1976 (W)		10/76
LA1030	City Tour 1976 (G)		10/76
LA1130	Silver Jubilee/Tour	1977	1978
LA1131	Silver Jubilee/Tour	1977	1978
LA1132	Silver Jubilee/Tour	1977	1978
LA1133	Silver Jubilee/Tour	1977	1978
LA1134	Silver Jubilee/Tour	1977	1978
LA1135	Bells Whisky	4/77	6/78
LA1142	Bells Whisky	5/77	6/78
LA1220	Open top Tours	5/78	
LA1239	Bells Whisky	6/78	7/79
LA1240	Bells Whisky	6/78	7/79

Fleet No.	Advert	From	To
LA1259	Barrowland Mrkt.	5/80	7/83
LA1262	City Tour	1979	1980
LA1263	City Tour	1979	1980
LA1264	City Tour	1979	1980
LA1266	Wellhall Garage	6/79	8/81
LA1293	Bells Whisky	6/79	5/81
LA1294	Bells Whisky	6/79	5/81
LA1304	LLoyds Bros.	7/79	6/81
LA1315	Stewart (hairdresser)	5/83	6/84
LA1351	Sony (videos)	11/81	6/82
LA1355	Devine (cycles)	11/81	11/84
LA1356	Maryhill Centre	4/82	5/83
LA1356	Whitehead (Dexion)	2/85	
LA1381	Chisholm & Hunter	12/82	8/83
LA1381	Anti-smoking	10/83	
LA1401	City Tour	1981	1985
LA1402	City Tour	1981	
LA1408	S.A.S. Airlines	12/85	
LA1411	Laing (Broadside)	2/84	
LA1412	Thomsons Stores	6/85	
LA1425	Henry Brothers	3/86	
LA1429	Sport for All	4/86	
LA1430	Stepek (Broadside)	9/84	5/86
LA1432	Wimpey Homes	4/85	
LA1435	Gold Centre	7/81	11/82
LA1436	Fostering Campaign	5/81	6/82
LA1437	Bells Whisky	6/81	5/83
LA1438	Bells Whisky	6/81	7/83
LA1438	Jolly Giant Toy Store	10/83	11/84
LA1441	Maryhill Carpets	7/82	12/83
A350	U'ground/Metric	1978	1984
L481	Local Govt. Reform	3/74	7/74
AV3	Leech Homes	5/82	6/84
AV16	Mad Buyer (store)	6/78	7/80
MB4	Asda Store	7/83	7/85
LO1	Drugs Abuse	7/85	
A34	Channel Four TV	11/82	5/83
A40	Terry's Chocolates	4/84	4/85
A40	N.W. Orient	6/85	
A66	BCC Scotland	1/83	4/85
A66	NW Orient	6/85	
A79	Bells Whisky	7/83	6/85
A80	Bells Whisky	7/83	6/85
A131	Bells Whisky	6/85	
A132	Bells Whisky	6/85	
LA1419	City Tour	1986	
SA1	Stakis Steakhouses	4/86	

The twenty Leyland Nationals of 1979 were delivered in all-over white and it was left to the PTE to add its own colour scheme, in this case, like the majority, yellow and verona green. LN16's screen shows 'Railway Emergency Service' as it travels eastwards along St. Vincent Street towards Queen Street Station on Inter-station service 98.

Service Vehicles

Registration No.	Make	Built	Converted	For use as	Scrapped
GB 6903	Halley P40	1924	1929	Breakdown lorry	?
GB 6906-7	Leyland GH7	1924	1929	Lorry	1939
GE 2434	Leyland TD1	1928	1935	Lorry	?
GE 2485	Leyland TD1	1928	1938	Mobile Canteen	?
GE 7270	Leyland TD1	1932	1933	Lorry (from chassis)	?
GE 7282	AEC Regent	1930	1941/2	Tow lorry	?
GG 2106	Leyland TD1	1930	1942	Tow lorry	1951
GG 7290	AEC Regent	1930	1946	Stop lorry	By 1970
GG 7291	AEC Regent	1930	1942	Tower Wagon	1960
GE 7288	AEC Regent	1930	1946	Tower Wagon	By 1968
CUS 802	AEC Regent	1939	1955	Mobile Workshop	By 1970
CUS 807	AEC Regent	1939	1955	Breakdown lorry	By 1970
CUS 815	AEC Regent	1939	1957	Crane Wagon	By 1970
DGB 388	AEC Regent	1940	1955	Mobile Workshop	?
T.P.	Leyland Hippo	1969	1976	Heavy Duty tow truck	
CGD 272K	Dodge	1972		Tow Wagon	
T.P.	Bedford			Tow Wagon/lorry	
FDS 281-2X	Bedford TL860	1982		Flat lorry	

AEC MATADOR		built 1947		Tow Wagon with Crane (covered lorry ★)	

	Scrapped		Scrapped		Scrapped
FGA 179 ★	1974	FYS 8	1981	FYS 10	1982
FYS 7	1982	FYS 9	1982		

AEC Regent		built 1939		converted 1959, 1961 ★, 1962 § Tow Wagon	

	Scrapped		Scrapped		Scrapped
BUS 167 ★	By 1970	BUS 176	1974	BUS 183	By 1970
BUS 169 ★	By 1970	BUS 179 §	1974	BUS 185 ★	1974
BUS 174 ★	By 1970	BUS 182	By 1970		

Leyland PD2/24		built 1959 (1960 ★)		converted 1970 (SGD 143 1975) Tow Wagon	

	Scrapped		Scrapped		Scrapped
SGD 259	1982	SGD 265	1982		
SGD 260	1982	SGD 266		SGD 289 ★	
SGD 261	1982	SGD 267			
SGD 262	1983	SGD 268	1984		
SGD 263	1982	SGD 269	1982	SGD 143	1982

Leyland PSU4A/4R	PSU3/3T ★	built 1971 (1965 ★)	converted 1981-2 Tow Wagon

DDB 157C ★	CHE 535K	CHE 540K
WHE 527J		

Demonstrating the righting of an overturned double-decker is AEC 'Matador' FYS 7 in its original condition and livery. It is probable that other service vehicles were painted in fleet livery for some part of their lives.

Allocation of Fleet at 1st February 1954

ELDERSLIE	AEC	A99, 105-112, 114, 116-7, 161, 217, 261, 265
	Daimler	114 (snow plough)
	Leyland	827-8 (19)

IBROX	AEC	A19-20, 54-5, 60-1, 91-3, 95-6, 100-4, 113, 115, 123, 131-2, 134-5, 139-43, 153-6, 162-3, 190, 196, 202, 208-13, 216, 218-22, 224-32, 236-8, 252-3, 255-6, 262-3: 583, 638, 750, 764-5 s.d. 705, 711-2
	Albion	B53-4, 64-5, 67-8, 71, 75, 78, 80, 82-3, 88-98, 110; BR10, 621
	Daimler	s.d. DS2, 3, 9, 17-18, 20, 22, 24-5, 27, 31, 34-7 (118)

HAMPDEN (Trolleybuses)	Daimler	147 snowplough, 156 (stored) (2)

KNIGHTSWOOD	AEC	A1-18, 21-53, 56-9, 94, 98, 118-22, 124-30, 136-8, 144-7, 149-52, 157-60, 164-6, 172-89, 197-201, 203-7, 214-5, 223, 233-5, 239-51, 254: 91-100, 549, 552, 555, 558, 566, 571, 573-5, 579, 586-7, 597, 649, 650, 652, 658, 724-6, 728-9, 731, 735-7, 741-2, 746, 748-9, 752, 755, 758-9, 761-2, 768-9, 770-1, 773: AR 266, 269-71, 276-7, 279, 283, 293-4, 296-7, 299-307: s.d. 693, 701-2, 717
	Albion	BS1
	Guy	68-9: 61-2, 66 (stored)
	Daimler	101, 104, 138-9, 158, 167 (stored): 129, 161-3 169 (Learner) s.d. DS5-8, 10-11, 13, 15-6, 21, 38-9, 41-4
	Leyland	L3-6, 8-9, 16-21, 23 (257)

LANGSIDE (Tram Depot)	Daimler	103, 128, 131, 134, 136, 140, 148, 153 (stored) (8)

LARKFIELD	AEC	A62-90, 97, 133, 148, 167-71, 191-5, 257-60, 264, AR267-8, 272-5, 278, 280-2, 284-92, 295, 308-10, 538-9, 542, 546, 548, 568, 598, 637, 639, 641-3, 646, 648, 651, 654, 657, 723, 733, 738, 740, 754, 760 (Learner) s.d. 694, 697, 698, 706, 722
	Albion	B18, 31-40, 42-9, 66, 70, 74, 114-6, 130-8: BR19, 21-7, 29
	Crossley	C1
	Daimler	D1-66: 115, 121, 159, 168; 102 (stored): 111, 149, 157, (Learner); 132-3, 143, 154-5 (Snowplough) s.d. DS14, 19, 23, 26, 28-30
	Leyland	L1-2, 7, 10-15, 22 (241)

PARKHEAD	Albion	B1-17, 19-30, 41, 50-2, 55-63, 69, 72-3, 76-7, 79, 81, 84-7, 99-109, 111-13, 117-129; BR1-9, 11-18, 20, 28, 30: 664, 774-83, 785-91, 810 s.d. 687-690, 692
	Daimler	s.d. DS1, 4, 12, 32-3, 40 (131)

30 vehicles at East Lancashire Coachbuilders for rebodying:-
105-110, 112-3, 116-8, 120, 122-7, 130, 135, 137, 141-2, 144-6, 150, 152, 165-6.

TOTAL FLEET 806

(Right) One of the appropriately registered pre-war AEC Regents, BUS 179, lingered on until 1974 after a total of 35 years' use. It is seen here at Govan outside the entrance to the pre-modernised 'Subway' with the staff canteen above. The exit was on the other side of Greenhaugh Street. A Leyland PD2/24 L78, on the service 34 (ex 4A) to Castlemilk is behind. Integration could not have been easier.